KEYS

TO

THE MESSIAH MYSTERY

A Resource Guidebook for "The Messiah Mystery"

by

Kay Bascom

ISBN: 0-9787175-1-1

DEDICATION

To those who have shared in the fellowship of the Messiah Mystery
and to those who hopefully will do so in the future,
this work is dedicated,
for God's glory.

ACKNOWLEDGMENTS

Bess Combs, a returned missionary from China, deeply touched our lives as new believers. Her life and teaching introduced hundreds of women and men to God's eternal purpose in classes that stressed a panoramic overview of the Messiah's presence throughout the Old and New Testaments. The Bible's "shadow and substance" metaphor, to which she alerted us, incubated in our minds over the years as we noticed the need for teaching that communicated the broad scope of the redemptive story.

Dr. Bascom's class on "The Messiah throughout the Scriptures" was asked for repeatedly, and eventually there was a request that it be put in written form. The book was named "The Messiah Mystery." Over the years with classes and friends in our local church and the Wellspring Fellowship, many of us experimented with creative ways of learning through a variety of Messiah-related celebrations. When Messiah Mystery classes needed a shorter form for time-limited classes, "Focus Pages" were created as a teaching alternative. Class members with a concern to teach a biblical overview began to gather their Shadow and Substance Circle diagrams, Focus Pages, and other handouts into a personal "Layered Teaching File" for future reference. This present booklet, "Keys to the Messiah Mystery," is an attempt to consolidate these basic teaching materials, adding templates for research, under one binding.

Many people have been involved in the metamorphosis that evolved into this guidebook. Shelly Potter Larkins first formatted the Shadow and Substance Circle diagrams. Kenny Lynch first formatted the "Focus Page" handouts. Now Alicia Goheen has made her computer designing skills available to create this bound collection of study aids, "Keys to the Messiah Mystery." The participation and prayers of class members and friends have been the inspiration behind the whole project, a product of a local body of Christ. Because our calling is to pass on the torch of Truth to every generation, we send these pages forth with prayer, hope, and thanksgiving.

Kay Bascom

KEYS TO THE MESSIAH MYSTERY
Resource Guidebook

CONTENTS

Table of Contents of "The Messiah Mystery"

INTRODUCTION

THE NEED FOR A PANORAMIC OVERVIEW Surrounded by our culture's sound-bite habits and smorgasbord-choice possibilities, even people desirous of spiritual pursuits can find their lives reduced to bits and pieces. We find ourselves floating in a distracted hodgepodge of activity, without focus. What can be of help when we cannot see the forest for the trees? Grasp of a unified picture of the whole is crucial. God has given us His ultimate meta-narrative in the Bible. Scripture records history over centuries and tells stories of great variety. Taking it as a whole, the word of God can become the gift that unifies our lives and puts us on the path to cooperation with the eternal purpose of our Creator God. "The Messiah Mystery" is an overview of that eternal purpose, with the Messiah as its unifying focus. It is unapologetically panoramic, in contrast to studies available in other modes, such as evangelistic, doctrinal, inductive, devotional, applicational, relational, etc. Each of these approaches is valuable, but a student of the Bible also needs a basic road map, a broad overview. Grasping a sense of the whole helps the parts become all the more meaningful.

THE BI-CULTURAL NECESSITY "The Messiah Mystery" takes a particularly Jewish look at the story of God's relationship to His people. Why? Because as the Master Teacher, God established a prototype, so that one community's sample of experience with Him could become a beachhead from which other communities could eventually profit. Every serious searcher after God needs to be bicultural. We all learn our own culture, but we need to learn something of the Hebrew culture to understand the message God has been so patiently and skillfully teaching over the ages. His teaching methods are fascinating! The scriptures are packed with truth in forms designed to reach all of us in every generation. He uses history, drama, stories, celebrations, sacred structures, sacred times, rituals, prophetic outworking, and more, all of which become keys to the mysterious meanings God has been unfolding. God's truth is worth finding, no matter how blurred the search has become in our relativistic, materialistic, post-modern, digitalized age. There is hope, for God is still going to have the last and most true word. May we enjoy it, and Him, early!

WHY A TEACHER'S RESOURCE GUIDEBOOK? The Messiah Mystery" is a long book, an unpopular form of study in our hurried, digital times. So why an addition? What are the "Keys to the Messiah Mystery" for? The Keys are a supplemental collection of underlying theoretical and practical materials designed to help individuals or groups study and/or teach the Messiah Mystery text. They may be copied and used in whatever way the user determines to be most helpful.

WHO MIGHT USE THE KEYS? The Keys provide resources that may be used in formal courses or informal studies, for personal or group study, in short or long sessions, with seekers or searchers. For those motivated to teach, the Keys can be used as tools to engage with a partner or a group in a study of the mystery of God's communication with us. The Keys are also an experiment in epistemology – noticing how God teaches humanity. They are meant to encourage creativity in those using them. As we employ some of the communication tools God created - our five senses, our minds, our hearts – we may become motivated to communicate what we are experiencing to others. Way down deep, the sons of Adam and daughters of Eve are thirsting to be filled with the Spirit of God and to be enfolded into His eternal purpose.

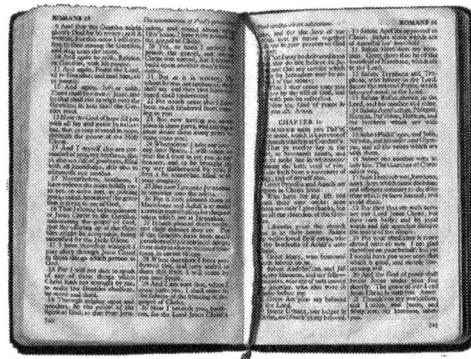

I. BASING YOUR STUDY ON GOD'S WORD:

THE CRUCIAL ROLE OF THE SCRIPTURES

This Section's Purpose:
    Since "The Messiah Mystery" is a panoramic survey of the Bible, being sure of the reliability of the scriptures is basic to the quest. Why can the biblical record be trusted? Where does its authority come from? Those who want to dig into the scriptures need to understand the basic presupposition underlying "The Messiah Mystery" and its accompanying "Keys to the Messiah Mystery."

THE BIBLE

Israel's scriptures record a vast *historical* drama

The Bible is God's message to the human race. Old Testament scripture spans the history of man from Creation to the Messiah's arrival, which the New Testament then records. The scriptures are basically *historical documents* based upon real lives in real places, which can be corroborated through archaeological and anthropological evidence. The more research is conducted by those disciplines, the more evidence is compiled for the reliability of the Judeo-Christian scriptures.

Historian Paul Johnson notes that the attention which the Bible has received exceeds by far that devoted to any other work in literature, and that this interest is not disproportionate, because it is the most influential of all books. He points out some unique characteristics of the Jewish people, for which the world has much to thank this record-keeping community:

> They were the first to create consequential, substantial and interpretative history . . . they knew they were a special people who had not simply evolved from an unrecorded past but had been brought into existence, for certain definite purposes, by a specific series of divine acts. They saw it as their collective business to determine, record, comment and reflect upon these acts. . . The Jews wanted to know about themselves and their destiny. They wanted to know about God and his intentions and wishes. Since God, in their theology, was the sole cause of all events – as Amos put it 'Does evil befall a city unless Yahweh wills it?' – and thus the author of history, and since they were the chosen actors in his vast dramas, the

record and study of historical events was the key to understanding of both God and man.[1]

Bible history is cast in an earthy mold of actual dates, events, and places in our physical environment - identifiable mountains, actual famines, recorded reigns of kings, etc. If we had only historical curiosity, we would find the study of the Bible eminently worth pursuing.

God is the source of the Bible's inspiration

The investigator naturally asks, "How can you trust the Bible to be reliable? Is it authentic, genuine?" One of the clues to its reliability and authorship is the fact that sixty-six books covering all time, recorded by around forty authors writing over a period of 1600 years, bring forth a unified message. This is only possible because *the message is all God's message,* dependent upon one source, God's Spirit, for its genesis and for its reliability. Unless God willed its inspiration, its writing, its protection, and its preservation, the Bible would not be. Nothing else like it exists,[2] for no one else could originate it or accomplish its production.

The Bible records God's intervention in the course of the sinful world's development, for the salvation of men otherwise lost, says Benjamin Warfield in his classic work on the inspiration and authority of the Bible. In Eden, the Lord God had been in fellowship with sinless man.

> This intimate association was broken up by the Fall. But God did not therefore withdraw Himself from concernment with men. Rather, He began at once a series of interventions in human history by means of which man might be rescued from his sin and, despite it, brought to the end destined for him. These interventions involved the segregation of a people for Himself, by whom God should be known, and whose distinction should be that God should be "nigh unto them" as He was not to other nations. (Deut. iv.7; Ps. cxlv.18).[3]

Warfield goes on to explain that "Jehovah chose Israel, not it Him," and that His choice rested not on their deserving, but on His gracious will.

> Nor was this people permitted to imagine that it was for its own sake alone that it had been singled out to be the sole recipient of the knowledge of Jehovah; it was made known from the beginning that God's mysteriously gracious dealing with it had as its ultimate end the blessing of the whole world (Gen. xii 2,3; xvii 4;5, 6;16, xviii 18; xxii 18; cf. Rom. iv.13), the bringing together again of the divided families of the earth under the glorious reign of Jehovah, and the reversal of the curse under which the whole world lay for its sin (Gen. xii.3).[4]

God revealed some of His attributes to all men through *nature*. Paul's introduction to the book of Romans says, "For what can be known about God is plain . . . Ever since the creation of the world his invisible nature, namely, his eternal power and deity, has been clearly perceived in the things that have been made." He revealed Himself personally to Israel through

---

[1] The History of the Jews, Paul Johnson (Harper and Row, Publishers, 1987) pg. 91, 92.

[2] The books of Islam and Mormonism resemble the biblical format and contain passages similar to the Bible, but they post-date the Bible, drawing from it and altering the previous original source. The Koran and the Book of Mormon were each produced by one individual.

[3] Benjamin Breckinridge Warfield, The Inspiration and Authority of the Bible (Presbyterian and Reformed Publishing Company, Philadelphia, Pennsylvania, 1948) p. 71.

[4] Warfield, pp. 71,72

special *revelation,* often called "grace." That revelation of grace was transferred from historical experience into written form through the inspired scriptures.

God does not attempt to verbally prove His own existence in the Bible. In his volume on the Pentateuch, C.H. Mackintosh points out the *lack* of argument for the existence of God in the book of Genesis. Genesis begins: "In the beginning, God created the heavens and the earth." The first sentence in the divine canon simply sets us in the presence of Him who is the infinite source of all true blessedness.

> There is no elaborate argument in proof of the existence of God. The Holy Ghost could not enter upon anything of the kind. God reveals Himself. He makes Himself known by His works. "The heavens declare the glory of God, and the firmament showeth His handiwork. . . .Great and marvelous are Thy works, Lord God Almighty." None but an infidel or an atheist would seek an argument in proof of the Being of One who, by the word of His mouth, called worlds into existence, and declared Himself the All-wise, the Almighty, and the everlasting God. Who but "God" could "create" anything? "Lift up your eyes on high, and behold who hath created these things, that bringeth out their host by number; He calleth them all by names, by the greatness of His might, for that He is strong in power; not one faileth.". . . In the book of Job (chap. 38-41) we have an appeal of the very grandest description, on the part of Jehovah Himself, to the work of creation, as an unanswerable argument in proof of His infinite superiority; and this appeal, while it sets before the understanding the most vivid and convincing demonstration of God's omnipotence, touches the heart also by its amazing condescension . . . tenderness . . .[5]

When asked for proof about Himself, God simply says, "Look around you; what do you see?" As He questioned ancient Job, "Where were you when I created the world?"

The scriptures themselves are God's testimony that He is not a remote "unmoved mover," but is deeply personal. He wills; He feels; He communicates. If He were not thus, we would have no Bible. Furthermore, God is the central actor in the human drama. This claims to be His story. The record proceeds, telling us many things about our predecessors as they cross earth's stage: Adam, Abraham, Moses, David - each generation has its day. And always, God communicates with man, in one way or another. When a prophet introduces a message with: "Thus saith the Lord," there is no question as to *Who* is speaking. The prophets paid a price for being the mouthpiece of God. On the eve of His departure from earth, Jesus wept over the holy city: "O Jerusalem, Jerusalem, killing the prophets and stoning those who are sent to you!" See His summary in Matthew 23:29-39.

THE LIVING WORD OF GOD AND THE BIBLE

Jesus' use of the Old Testament

The reliability of the Old Testament message is further substantiated by the Messiah's use of it. The attitude of the Lord Jesus Christ toward the scriptures authenticates the Old Testament for Christians. His use of the scriptures indicates a solid acceptance of their veracity. It would be senseless for people who trust Christ as the representative of God to question *His* judgment.

---

[5] Genesis to Deuteronomy, C. H. Mackintosh (Louizeaux Brothers, reprinted in 1972 - from the 1880's) p. 17.

Jesus Christ lived in obedience to the Old Testament, and taught submission to the authority of Israel's scriptures – not to "the commandments of men" – but to the Old Testament word of God. In the Sermon on the Mount in Matthew 5, Jesus affirms:

> Think not that I have come to abolish the law and the prophets; I have come not to abolish them but to fulfill them. For truly, I say to you, till heaven and earth pass away, not an iota, not a dot, will pass from the law until all is accomplished.

His message dovetails with the law and the prophets. He came to accomplish, fulfill, and complete what they began.

In the New Testament we can examine how Jesus used the Old Testament scriptures. When under attack, He answered Satan during the temptation (recorded in Luke 4) in the wilderness each time with scriptures, saying, "It is written . . ." When teaching, over and over He quoted scripture as His authority. When questioned by adversaries, He responded with counter-questions showing His own rule of faith: "What is written in the law?"[6] When facing His passion, He accepted it as necessary for the Messiah's fulfillment of scripture. When Peter could not understand His non-resistance to arrest, Jesus flatly stated the necessity of scripture's being fulfilled:

> Put your sword back into its place . . . Do you think I cannot appeal to my Father and he will at once send me more than twelve legions of angels? But how then should the scriptures be fulfilled, that it must be so? (Matthew 26:52-54)

When His identity or mission was questioned, Jesus applied the messianic scriptures to Himself, both before and after His death. Two people on the road to Emmaus that first night after the resurrection heard the risen Lord's own exposition of His presence in the Old Testament when, "beginning with Moses and all the prophets, he interpreted to them in all the scriptures the things concerning himself."! (Luke 24:27)

Jesus is the New Testament's message and is its guarantor

The Gospels record the fulfillment of those "scriptures concerning Himself," giving us records of the Messiah's appearance on earth. The Gospel's authority arises from the very One whose story it tells, "the Son of God." If He is not truly God, then His word about things cannot be supremely trusted. His *identity* is the foundation upon which the New Testament's claim to inspiration and reliability is built. The New Testament and Jesus' claim to Godhood stand or fall together.

John speaks of Jesus as the very word of God become incarnate. Words are tools for communication. *Jesus is God's communication* to earth, so He is called "the Word of God." John's Gospel begins:

> In the beginning was *the Word*, and *the Word* was with God, and *the Word* was God. He was in the beginning with God; all things were made through him, and without him was not anything made that was made. In him was life, and the life was the light of men. . . . He was in the world, and the world was made through him, yet the world knew him not. He came to his own home, and his own people received him not. But to all who received him, who believed in his name, he gave power to become children of God; . . . And *the Word* became flesh and dwelt

---

[6] Luke 10:26a. Note that while Jesus used the scriptures continually, He warned that they could not give eternal life apart from Himself. "You search the scriptures, because you think that in them you have eternal life; and it is they that bear witness to me; yet you refuse to come to me that you may have life." John 5: 39,40.

among us, full of grace and truth; we have beheld his glory, glory as of the only Son from the Father . . . For the law was given through Moses; grace and truth came through Jesus Christ. No one has ever seen God; the only Son, who is in the bosom of the Father, *he has made him known.*[7]

In quoting Jesus, the New Testament writers' presupposition is that they are quoting God's Son! Such a claim has to be either blasphemy or truth.

THE APOSTLES' WITNESS AFTER THE ASCENSION

The concluding half of the New Testament

Following the biographical material in the four Gospels, the last half of the New Testament reports the period after Christ's ascension from earth. It includes the historical record of the Acts of the apostles, a number of letters to the infant churches and to individuals, and the closing prophetic Book of Revelation. These portions of scripture focus upon *the mystery of the Messiah* that was hidden in past times and is coming to light. They write about *the mystery of the emerging church* – a Jew/Gentile phenomenon. The author of these documents is the Holy Spirit, the Third Person of the Triune God, who gave birth to the church, just as Christ promised at His departure.[8]

The Acts and the Letters were recorded under the inspiration of the Spirit in the middle of the first century AD, while the Church was taking form. Acts records what happened; it could be called "the acts of the Holy Spirit through the apostles." In the letters we read the counsel given to the young congregations or pastors in the midst of their on-going lives. The closing book, Revelation, is an apocalyptic vision of the future, addressed to seven of those churches. Revelation chapter 4 begins to open up to human view "what must take place after this."

The authority of the apostles' message

To what did the writers of the New Testament attribute their authority to record these things, claiming "inspiration"? To answer that, we must understand one important fact. Jesus promised the *indwelling* presence of the Holy Spirit as His parting gift. He said the Spirit would dwell not only *with* but soon would take up residence *in* His people. Jesus assured the disciples that the person of the Holy Spirit would "guide them into all truth" and "bring to their remembrance" all that He had said to them. Their Lord talked with them about this crucial promise during His last night with them, recorded in John 14-16. The Holy Spirit is rightly called the author – perhaps some would say "the managing editor" – of the New Testament.

As they worded the messages given them by the Spirit, the apostolic writers were in unity with God's message given throughout the centuries and through the Son. They recorded these things during their own unique time on earth. Says John in the opening of his first Letter:

That which we have seen and heard we proclaim also to you, so that you may have fellowship with us; and our fellowship is with the Father and with his Son Jesus Christ. . . . This is the message we have heard from him and proclaim to you . . .

They saw the divine plan as an offer of fellowship from the Father through the Son to them, and by the Spirit's activity, sent on out to the world.

---

[7] John 1:1-5; 10-12, 14,17,18. Reader, please note the author's frequent addition of italics to emphasize some aspect.

[8] See Acts 1:8, fulfilled in Acts 2:1-4.

Their message is claimed as trustworthy primarily because of the inspiration of the Holy Spirit by which they spoke, and to whom they testified:

> First of all you must understand this, that no prophecy of scripture is a matter of one's own interpretation, because no prophecy ever came by the impulse of man, but *men moved by the Holy Spirit spoke from God.* (II Peter 1:20,21)

Such a claim is either true or false. And if the Holy Spirit actually did move men to speak from God, then no one is more "reliable" than God the Spirit.

Secondly, the apostles' reliability rested upon their own credentials. Jesus had many disciples, but He chose from them twelve, whom He named "apostles." An apostle is "one sent," commissioned, not self-appointed. Christ said He did not speak on His own authority, but from the Father, the apostles also did not speak on their own authority, but from Jesus. John R. W. Stott explains:

> When the time came to settle the canon of the New Testament and in particular which books should be excluded, the supreme question about every question-marked book was whether it possessed apostolic authority. Had it been written by an apostle? If not, did it carry the imprimatur of apostles in that it came from their circle and represented their teaching? The test of canonicity was apostolicity.[9]

The apostles knew that questions would reasonably be raised by their claim to be delivering a divine message. Probably no one was more serious about being sure of their veracity than they were, themselves. Their letters contained passages like Peter's statement of purpose in writing his letters:

> I think it right, as long as I am in this body, to arouse you by way of reminder, since I know that the putting off of my body will be soon, as our Lord Jesus Christ showed me. And I will see to it that after my departure you may be able at any time to recall these things. For we did not follow cleverly devised myths when we made known to you the power and coming of our Lord Jesus Christ, but we were eyewitnesses of his majesty. (II Peter 1:13-16)

The apostles saw to it that the first-hand record of eyewitnesses be made available for future generations. They trusted God in this divine task.

Assuaging Jewish fears about the New Testament

Those of the Jewish community who have not looked into the New Testament may assume it carries a depreciating attitude toward the Old Covenant scriptures. Quite to the contrary, Christians look upon the Old Testament as equally inspired as the New. After all, the Old comprises three-fourths of what God chose to inspire as scripture. The Old Covenant is the foundation of Christianity, the preparation for which the Messiah is the agent of consummation.

Often Jewish people react to the New Testament's use of the term, "the Jews." Conditioned by fear of anti-Semitism, accusers sometimes appeal to these passages, viewing them as if Gentiles wrote them, and as if they were written in modern times. We must remember that Jesus was Jewish, and His followers were nearly all Jews. In the Gospels we are hearing history – Jews talking about Jews. Even when Paul's letters speak of his message being rejected by "the Jews," we must remember that Paul is himself a Jew (even a Pharisee) talking about Jews – about the religiously powerful Jews, the Jews that largely rejected Jesus.

---

[9] The Authority of the Bible, John R.W. Stott, (InterVarsity Christian Fellowship, 1974) p. 26.

But always the New Testament says, "the common people [i.e. the *also Jewish* people] heard him gladly." (Mark 12:37 KJV)

The glorified Jesus closes the scriptures

Some ask why the scripture canon closed, limiting scripture to what had been written in the first century. When the Messiah's mission was accomplished, further scripture was unnecessary. The book of Revelation seals the message of salvation, and shows as much of the future and eternity as God chose to reveal.

The early Christians were very careful not to alter or add to God's chosen message. John Stott quotes Tertullian, who wrote about 200 AD:

> We Christians are forbidden to introduce anything on our own authority, or to choose what someone else introduces on his own authority. Our authorities are the Lord's apostles, and they in their turn choose to introduce nothing on their own authority. They faithfully passed on to the nations the teaching which they had received from Christ.[10]

God's message to man reached its consummation in the Messiah. The Old Testament had prepared for what the New then fulfilled. The Promised One had come and been proclaimed. Even those sweeping judgments and events that would complete the promises in the future were already prophesied in the book of Revelation. The last word necessary had been said.

And so the Bible comes to a close in the name of the Messiah himself, "and the name by which he is called is The Word of God." (Revelation 13:19b) He identifies Himself: "I am the Alpha and the Omega, the first and the last, the beginning and the end. . . . I am the root and the offspring of David, the bright morning star." (Revelation 22:13;16)

THE HOLY SPIRIT CONTINUES TO LIFT UP JESUS

The pragmatic test of truth

When one is dealing with spiritual things, proof in the "litmus paper" sense is not a possible category. We cannot do a chemical test to prove the existence of "faith" or "hope" or "love." An hypothesis is corroborated by testing it. While a truth cannot be proven, it can be tested for reality. We can evaluate how well it matches the hard facts of life. Because Christians believe scripture is the inspired word of God and the supreme authority for their lives, they test it out, to see how well it matches up with the facts of history and the daily realities of living. Does it hold up or not? Can lives really resonate with the scriptures?

Millions say, " Yes!" Over these long years of devotion to the holy scriptures, people in hundreds of nations, from dozens of races, educated and uneducated, rich and poor, have valued and trusted scripture as the supreme guide for understanding and living life. They do not trust the Bible itself, as one would trust a text; they trust (i.e. have personal confidence in) the *author* of the Bible, the Holy Spirit. The testimony of these many lives is one argument for the reliability of the Bible.

Those who do not just read it but submit themselves to the word of God, come to *know* its power, for they are laid bare by it, collide with it, are transformed by it. Of itself scripture says, "The word of God is living and active; sharper than any two-edged sword, piercing to the

---

[10] Prescriptions against Heretics, Tertullian, chapter 6, quoted by Stott.

division of soul and spirit, of joints and marrow, and discerning the thoughts and intentions of the heart." (Hebrews 4:12)

The Messiah is the cornerstone of the Spirit's message

Finally, the incarnated, flesh-and-blood Messiah is the cornerstone of the Bible. He is the One from whom all emanates, to whom all are responsible, and in whom all treasures are hid.

The New Testament is the record of the Messiah's being manifested *in the flesh.* The early writings warn that ". . . many deceivers have gone out into the world, men who will not acknowledge the coming of Jesus Christ *in the flesh* . . . " (II John 7a) After the resurrection, when Jesus startled the disciples with His appearance by walking right into their room, He said: "See my hands and my feet, that it is I myself; handle me, and see; for a spirit has not *flesh and bones* as you see that I have." (Luke 24:39,40) The Messiah is not simply a godly man, not an angel, not an avatar, but the bodily-resurrected living and eternal Lord of heaven and earth. In a "nutshell" summary of the New Testament message in I Corinthians 15:3-8, Paul insists upon flesh-and-blood historicity:

> For I delivered to you as of first importance what I also received, that Christ *died* for our sins in accordance with the scriptures, that he was *buried,* that he was *raised* on the third day in accordance with the scriptures, and that he *appeared* to Cephas, then to the twelve. Then he *appeared* to more than five hundred brethren at one time, most of whom are still alive, though some have fallen asleep. Then he *appeared* to James, then to all the apostles. Last of all, as to one untimely born, he *appeared* also to me.

Physical death, burial, resurrection. Visible, touchable, verifiable. This is what the Spirit testifies to, in the scriptures. The Spirit breathes that witness into the lives of believers day by day over the centuries.

Our mandate today

This explanation touches only the surface of what could be said about the authenticity of the message of the Bible. Some come to the scriptures to decide whether to believe. Others have believed, and wish to help others find their way. The Bible speaks for itself, but often people are unwilling to give it a hearing without developing at least a partial trust in the reliability of the Bible. The lives of faithful Christians constitute the best argument for what the Bible produces. If a believer's life inspires a searcher to ask questions about our Savior and Lord, then our personal testimony, the scriptures themselves, and the apologetical resources we are alert to supply, can all be helpful.

Since sources are crucial in the pursuit of truth, a believer has the responsibility to offer to questioners solid arguments for the Bible's reliability. The footnotes suggest a few helpful resources.[11] Bible handbooks for lay use usually include brief summaries and archaeological and historical evidences for the Bible's authenticity.[12] Josh McDowell's Evidence Which Demands a Verdict,[13] which has been used all over the world, is a case in point for the

---

[11] A few references on the authenticity of the Bible: F. F. Bruce's short The New Testament Documents: Are They Reliable? (Eerdman's Publishing Company, 1959); Carl F. H. Henry's four-volume God, Revelation and Authority (Word Books, Publisher, 1976-1980); J. I. Packer's God Has Spoken (InterVarsity Press, 1979); Josh McDowell's books: see footnote 36.

[12] Halley's Bible Handbook (Zondervan Publishing House, 1965) and The New Unger's Bible Handbook (Moody Press, 1984) are brief handbooks for laymen. A number of more extensive handbooks are available. Book-by-book commentaries provide additional in-depth material.

[13] Evidence Which Demands a Verdict, Josh McDowell, (Here's Life Publishers, 1979). A rich apologetical resource focused upon the biblical record itself is his Evidence Which Demands a Verdict, Vol. 2. (Published

enhancement of receptivity that comes from facing the issues of apologetics with preparedness and skill.

Often, however, the human problem is the absence of honest *willingness* to face truth, even when its integrity is demonstrated. As we try to be prepared to "give an answer for the hope that is in us," we are admonished to do it with "gentleness and reverence." (I Peter 3:15) The word of God is given to us for this task. "All scripture is given by inspiration of God, and is profitable for doctrine, for reproof, for correction, for instruction in righteousness." (II Timothy 3:16) God's people are themselves to be transformed by the scriptures, so that the world may believe that the Father sent the Son. Let us remember that it is not the argument but the person that God desires to win. No matter how reasonable truth is, truth is impersonal. Love is not; love is personal. It is God's love through His people that can open hearts to truth.

---

originally as <u>More Evidence Which Demands a Verdict</u> by Here's Life Publishers in 1975 and 1981, and re-published as <u>Evidence Which Demands a Verdict: Volume 2</u> by Thomas Nelson, 1993).

THE MESSIAH: Preparation & Consummation

SUBSTANCE

New Testament

Colossians 2:17

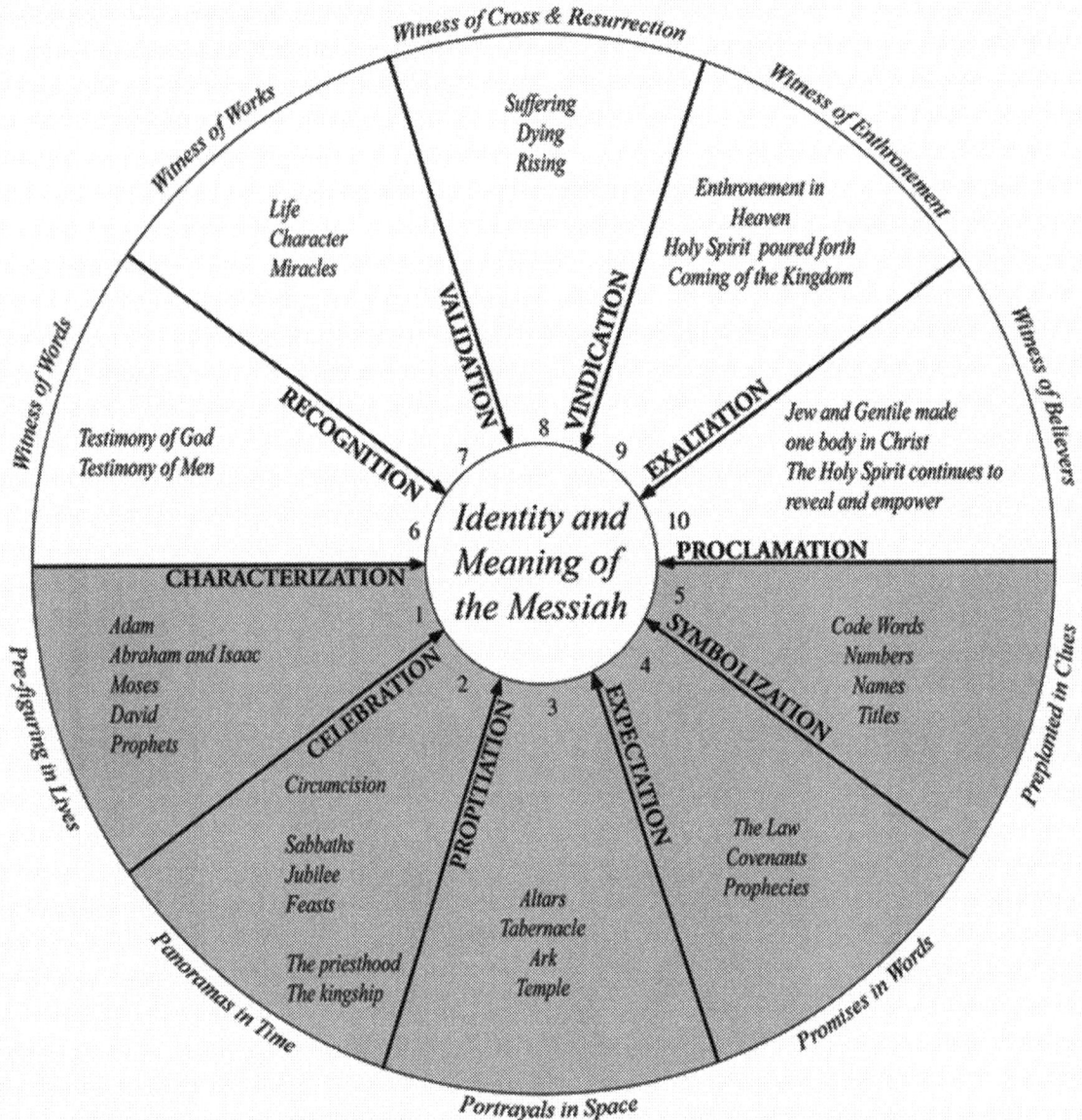

Witness of Cross & Resurrection

Witness of Works

Witness of Enthronement

Suffering
Dying
Rising

Life
Character
Miracles

Enthronement in
Heaven
Holy Spirit poured forth
Coming of the Kingdom

Witness of Words

VALIDATION

VINDICATION

Witness of Believers

RECOGNITION

EXALTATION

Testimony of God
Testimony of Men

7   8   9

Jew and Gentile made
one body in Christ
The Holy Spirit continues to
reveal and empower

6

*Identity and
Meaning of
the Messiah*

10   PROCLAMATION

CHARACTERIZATION

5

Pre-figuring in Lives

Adam
Abraham and Isaac
Moses
David
Prophets

1

CELEBRATION

2   3   4

SYMBOLIZATION

Code Words
Numbers
Names
Titles

Preplanted in Clues

Circumcision

PROPITIATION

EXPECTATION

The Law
Covenants
Prophecies

Sabbaths
Jubilee
Feasts

Altars
Tabernacle
Ark
Temple

Panoramas in Time

The priesthood
The kingship

Promises in Words

Portrayals in Space

SHADOW

Old Testament

Hebrews 8:5, 10:1

II. GRASPING A PANORAMIC BIBLICAL OVERVIEW

THE "SHADOW AND SUBSTANCE" METHOD

This Section's Purpose:
"The Messiah Mystery" uses a concept of study that can be termed a "shadow and substance" method. The scriptures use these terms to compare and contrast the shadowy "patterns" and "types" that God initiated in the Old Testament and the realities He brought to fulfillment in the Messiah's arrival. The Bible gives us a sense of God's overview from Eternity, in contrast to our limited concepts within Time. Our Creator's eternal perspective is not available anywhere else except in God's word.

CONCEPTUALIZING THE MESSIANIC STORY

Seedbed

From *man's viewpoint*, the Bible records a developmental process. We can look at the earliest scriptures as the "seedbed" of the Bible. That is, Genesis and Exodus particularly are full of first-time happenings, "seeds" that are taking root: creation . . . man and woman . . . the Fall . . . sacrifice . . . murder . . . the flood . . . the call of Abraham . . . circumcision . . . the exodus . . . law . . . tabernacle. As the story of mankind moves onward, seeds sown in the early years begin to grow, to reproduce, to bring forth fruit, for good or for ill. Tracing the growth of these "seeds" can tell us much about life, man, and God.

The special perspective of "The Messiah Mystery's" *panoramic* study method is *overview*, and calls for a broad search. A "seed" idea can be traced (using a Bible concordance) to see whether it is representative of God's overall message, and can be found throughout both Testaments of the Bible. Major seed ideas amplify and sharpen God's message to man.

From shadow to substance

From *God's vantage point,* certain spiritual realities necessarily must be brought to dawn upon the mind of finite man slowly, moving out of the mist, or shadows, into full light. An illustration which proves valuable for this panoramic search would be to call it a "shadow and substance" way of looking at scripture. The terms "shadow" and "substance" come from the New Testament book written to the Hebrews, which reflects a particularly Jewish way of looking at the history of God's dealings with mankind.[14] The early happenings were seen as

---

[14] See Hebrews 8:5, 9:23,24; 10:1.

"shadows" of what would eventually appear "in substance" on earth, yet having been solid realities in eternity all along.

To use a literal example, as one walks toward the sun, a shadow of whatever is standing up ahead (like a tree) falls *toward the one walking forward.* As the world walks toward the fulfillment of history, it walks within the shadow of the reality up ahead. Because eternal things are forever (in a sense the divine "tree" has stood there all along), the reality of that "tree" on which the Messiah was crucified always was throwing its shadow from eternity *toward or into time.* We must consider that God is outside of time and is able to see the end from the beginning. What is in His eternal "now" can best be explained to finite beings as *finished* "before the foundation of the world."[15] Therefore scripture speaks of Christ's blood as "shed from the foundation of the world"[16] or of "the Lamb slain from the foundation of the world."[17]

A shadow can be traced to its source. We can either move forward from the Old Testament toward the "substance" which cast its shadow backward; or, conversely, we can move backward from the New Testament, observing each long shadow which has cast its particular shape across the lives of our spiritual forefathers, during the Old Testament period of "foreshadowing."

The letter written to the first-century Hebrew Christians especially employs the concept of shadow and substance. Jews comprised the majority of the early Church at that time. There was a need to explain the relationship between the *newness* brought in by the advent of the Messiah and the *oldness* of the Jewish sacrifices. The book of Hebrews provides this picture:

> For since the law has but a *shadow* of the good things to come instead of the *true form* of these realities, it can never, by the same sacrifices which are continually offered year after year, make perfect those who draw near. Otherwise, would they not have ceased to be offered?[18]

In speaking of the priesthood and sacrifices of the Old Covenant system, Hebrews says that since the advent of the Messiah,

> . . . we have such a high priest, one who is seated at the right hand of the throne of the Majesty in heaven, a minister in the sanctuary and *the true tent* which is set up not by man but by the Lord. . . . They [the Levitical priests] serve a *copy and shadow* of the *heavenly sanctuary,* for when Moses was about to erect the tent, he was instructed by God, saying, "See that you make everything according to the pattern which was shown you on the mountain." . . . Indeed, under the law almost everything is purified with blood, and without the shedding of blood there is no forgiveness of sins. Thus it was necessary for the *copies* of the heavenly things to be purified with these rites, but the *heavenly things themselves* with better sacrifices than these. For Christ has entered, not into a sanctuary made with hands, a *copy* of the *true* one, but into heaven itself, now to appear in the presence of God on our behalf.[19]

---

[15] See Matthew 13:35, John 17:24, etc.

[16] See Luke 11:50.

[17] See Revelation 13:8, KJV.

[18] Hebrews 10:1,2. The word used for "shadow" here gives the sense of outline or image.

[19] Hebrews 8:1b,2,5; 9:22-25

It must be understood that the expressions "copies" or "shadows" do not denigrate or nullify the importance of the early Tabernacle, "the tent." On the contrary, the sacrificial system provided the foundation for interpreting the meaning of the Messiah's role – that of being the final and perfect Great High Priest, as well as the final and perfect sacrificial Lamb of God. Through the day-by-day and year-by-year sacrificial system of the Tabernacle and Temple, God indelibly demonstrated to the Hebrews that sin brings forth the requirement of a death penalty – either their own death, or the death of God's mercifully provided substitute. Without the Old Testament preparation, we could not have understood the significance of the Messiah's sacrifice.

"Do your best ... rightly handling the word of truth"

God's part has been to reveal. Ours is to receive His message. Paul advised Timothy, "Do your best to present yourself to God as one approved, a workman who has no need to be ashamed, rightly handling the word of truth."[20] The King James translation says, "rightly dividing the word of truth." Perhaps that is partially what is being attempted in dividing scriptures into Old and New, shadow and substance, various covenants, dispensations, etc. Such divisions reflect periods in *time*. Other ways to "divide" the limitless truth into digestible pieces is to look, say, at *content* – biographies, parables, psalms, doctrines, etc. These are grasp-able handles to help us hold on to the word of God.

THE "SHADOW AND SUBSTANCE" DIAGRAM

1. Interpreting the diagram

The "Shadow and Substance" method used in this book is a *tool* for tracking though the whole Bible. It incorporates a number of layers of meanings: historical progression, old and new covenant comparisons and distinctions, typology in lives and other metaphorical aspects, prophetic connections, biographical facts, personal testimonies, etc.

It will be well to look at the circle pictured in the Shadow and Substance master diagram printed at the beginning of Part II of this "Keys" text, and on page 49 of "The Messiah Mystery." The twelve sections of the Messiah Mystery study each have a diagram printed here in the Keys in Part III, Alternative A. The S and S concept is also presented on a single page (with accompanying Master S and S Circle diagram) for those using the Focus Page method of teaching, in Part III, Alternative C. All of the circles may be copied for educational use.

a. Two halves of the circle

In the diagram, the first differentiation is a shaded lower half and a clear upper half of the circle. (It is introduced in the Abraham section of the book.) The two parts are differentiated to demonstrate the "shadow" and "substance" periods in *time*, i.e. the Old and New Testaments. Shadow and substance go together as two parts of a whole, becoming co-revelatory. A shadow is non-existent without a source, and is dependent upon and intrinsically connected to its source. Conversely, shadows delineate major outlines of their source.

b. The center and ten sections around the circumference

The circle has a center, which represents the identity and meaning of the Messiah. It is as if the Messiah stands in the spotlight on center stage of a "theater in the round." Imagine Jesus on a platform at the center of a great coliseum. For the student, each section of the stadium represents a different area to analyze, all bearing some crucial relationship to the Messiah.

---

[20] II Timothy 2:15

Titles for the ten sections are written on the circle's circumference:

Old Testament	New Testament
1. Prefiguring in lives	6. Witness of words
2. Panoramas in time	7. Witness of works
3. Portrayals in space	8. Witness of cross, resurrection
4. Promises in words	9. Witness of enthronement
5. Pre-planted in clues	10. Witness of believers

Within the sections, you will see further refinements. For instance, in section one, called "Prefiguring in lives," certain lives are listed: "Adam, Abraham, Moses, David, etc." The topics written inside each section are key words for the study within the section. As one learns to use this method, such topics could be expanded.

c. Ten pointers: summary words for each section's *function*

The ten angled pointers toward the Messiah in the center simply *restate the subject matter (designated on the circumference) in terms of function.* What does each section *do* in relationship to the One on trial on the world's stage?

Going around the lower <u>shadow</u> sections 1-5, left to right, (counter-clockwise) from the "pre-figuring in lives" section, various *characterizations* pointing to the Messiah can be gleaned. The "panoramas in time" (like the weekly sabbath, or yearly feasts) function as *celebrations* pointing to the Messiah. The "portrayals in space" (in the Tabernacle and Temple) involve *propitiation* pointing to the Messiah. The "promises in words" (like covenants and prophecies) are statements of *expectations* pointing to the coming Messiah. The pre-planted clues (like titles, names, numbers, code-words) transfer meanings by *symbolization* of the meaning of the Messiah.

Then we start at the left-most section of the upper circle and move clockwise through sections 6-10 worded with five forms of witness on the circumference. Functions are printed on the angled pointers. In the New Testament period, shadow has become <u>substance</u> in the arrival of the Messiah. When He came, both God and man witnessed verbally to who He was, providing us with helps for our own *recognition* of His identity. Jesus' works – His way of living, His healing the sick, cleansing the leper, exorcising the possessed, creating elements of wine and bread, commanding nature, raising the dead – provided *validation* of who He was. Then He suffered, died, was buried and raised, all a witness in that He fulfilled the messianic prophecies. His resurrection became the *vindication* before His accusers, pronounced and accomplished by God Himself. As a testimony to the Messiah's enthronement in heaven, the Holy Spirit was poured out, announcing Christ's *exaltation.* The believers (both Jews and Gentiles who received Him as their Lord and king) went forth in *proclamation* of the good news of God's Messiah to the world.

2. Shadow and Substance Method also like a conceptual "magnet"
Some might understand this method of study in possibly more dynamic terms if conceived of as a *"magnetic attraction" process.* Picture a horseshoe-shaped magnet with one pole placed upon the highly-charged Messiah in the center of the illustration, the other pole placed upon some aspect under consideration.

For example, let's try one of the "code words" in the "pre-planted clues" section (number 5, to the far right of the shadow half), the word "lamb." This word can be found from Genesis to Revelation. Place one pole on the Messiah in the center and sweep the magnet's other pole around the whole circle. Those filings (as of steel) magnetized by "lamb" that somehow match the pull of the *"Messiah-as-lamb magnet"* jump up onto it from various passages all throughout the scriptures.

Filings "match" not because they happen to use the right *words* (which could be artificial, manipulative, or a foolish forcing of the scripture), but because they authentically match in *meaning*. Sometimes the match is obvious. Sometimes we have to be enlightened by being told that they match, by the Holy Spirit's connecting the two somewhere in scripture. For example, Peter at Pentecost was inspired to say, ". . . *this is that* which was spoken by the prophet Joel . . ."[21] When the Ethiopian official asked Philip who Isaiah 53 referred to, Philip immediately equated the "sheep led to the slaughter" with the Lamb who had just been slain. So, "beginning with *this scripture* he told him the good news of Jesus."[22]

If you choose any magnetized aspect or role of the Messiah and then sweep from left to right through the Old Testament, you will pick up various kinds of information (historical and interpretive) out of *the Old Testament period of foundation and preparation.* Then, starting at the top half circle, and sweeping from left to right through the New Testament witness, you will pick up what matches the Old from *the New Testament's perspective of fulfillment and consummation.*

AN INSIGHTFUL METAPHOR FOR WHAT THE BIBLE IS MEANT TO DO FOR US

As we search, it is crucial to be clear on the major purpose of the Bible. What is the intended role of the scriptures? Donald Mostrum in Intimacy with God insists that "the unique power of the Bible lies in the fact that God sovereignly associates Himself with His word. He reveals Himself by Scripture; He doesn't just issue data about Himself. He actively uses it as His instrument to create a relationship with Himself." Here is a keen analogy from Mostrum's book:

> Imagine yourself on a cold day outside a large window. The heat of the room within has steamed up the window, and as you come close, you realize that someone has written with his finger on the inside of the window. You stand there reading what has been printed. Your eyes are focused on the writing. But suddenly you become aware that you can see through the writing to the room beyond, and a person, presumably the writer, is standing immediately behind the window. Your sudden change of attitude is something like what happens as God confronts us with His living presence when we thought we were just looking at the words of Scripture.[23]

As we begin to trace the Messiah's presence through the scriptures, may the face of God become more visible "behind the window." Yet God is spirit and cannot be physically seen by man. How wonderful that He spanned that gap by making Himself visible by the Incarnation. "Jesus cried out and said, 'He who believes in me, believes not in me but in him who sent me. And he who sees me sees him who sent me . . . He who has seen me has seen the Father.' "[24] Shocking! Amazing. Response unavoidable.

---

[21] Acts 2:16, quoting from Joel 2:28-31
[22] See Acts 8:26-40.
[23] Intimacy with God, Donald G. Mostrom (Tyndale House Publishers, 1984) pg. 23.
[24] John 12:44,45; 14:9b

III. STUDYING IN ALTERNATIVE MODES:

INTRODUCTION TO CHOOSING A METHOD

This Section's Purpose:
Because "The Messiah Mystery" hits high points throughout the whole Bible, it is a study that can be begun and reviewed and repeated in a number of ways. Some have read the book, and then done the study again, using one of the alternatives suggested in this section. Sensing the universal need for a panoramic overview of the Bible, some have become motivated to pass it on. The materials in this section are a collection of ways to share the material, from which a leader can choose.

THE GUIDE'S DECISION ON HOW TO APPROACH THE STUDY Which of the approaches below may better fit the leader's teaching style, or a proposed group's make up, or its size, or its time frame? How committed is a given group to studying in depth? Are the participants in a formal class for credit, or in an informal study? What alternative will fit the situation best? A guide can be creative in how to lead a group through this adventure. God's truth is to be passed on, and these Keys are just one set of tools for doing so. Below are three main study modes that have been developed.

ALTERNATIVE A:
Individual study can be based on "The Messiah Mystery" book, centering primarily on scripture research, using the S and S Circle diagrams. They are printed here in Part III of the Keys, Alternative A.

ALTERNATIVE B:
The simplest way for a group to study the biblical overview covered in "The Messiah Mystery" is to read the text and use the discussion questions available at the end of each chapter. The Keys also include those questions here in Part III Alternative B.

ALTERNATIVE C:
Some class time slots may not allow for long sessions. For briefer group sessions whose participants do not necessarily use the long text, the Keys provide one-page summaries of the 24 chapter topics, called "Focus Pages."

TOOLS: The following pages in Part III provide explanations and tools for using these modes of study. *Master copies and templates are provided, with permission to copy them.

ALTERNATIVE A:

INDIVIDUAL BOOK STUDY FOCUSED ON S AND S CIRCLES

The twelve topical Shadow and Substance Circles for "The Messiah Mystery" can be a basis of research for individuals or partners, who, like the Bereans in Acts 17, "searched the scriptures daily to see whether these things were so." Leaders will especially find their own circle research to be a basic resource, even if they use one of the other modes for teaching.

USES OF THE "S AND S" CIRCLES

1. Introducing the Concept:
The Master Circle helps conceptualize a look at biblical history and experience from God's viewpoint, from "above." It looks down, so to speak, on a "theater in the round" – or on an stadium with spectator sections that represent a sweep through the Old and New Testament communities' experiences.

2. Learning from the Master Teacher's Methods:
The 10 sections of the "S and S" circles draw attention to God's way of teaching humanity. They dramatize the problem of communication between God and man. His masterfully creative ways of teaching can inform and enhance our own, as we become conduits of His message.

3. Guiding the Research:
The 12 circles each focus on one theme of the Bible. The searcher may sweep (like using a magnet) across the scriptures to collect a sample of "gleanings" from each section. The categories help us remember them. Students may be motivated to add their own findings. Keeping this research in personal files can be useful when needed in the future. A template for preserving research is printed at the end of this section.

4. Disciplining the Mind and Heart:
Often simplicity is the key to summarizing and retaining concepts. An introduction and a set of Key Scriptures matching the Messiah Mystery topics are printed here in Part III A. Their thoughtful memorization can be of assistance in grasping meanings, transferring these concepts to others, and conserving the effort invested in the study of "The Messiah Mystery."

TOOLS:
1. Diagrams of the twelve Shadow and Substance Circle diagrams.
2. A blank template for multiple copies on which to record personal research on any circle.
3. A "Hand" introduction, and 15 Key Scriptures from "The Messiah Mystery," for memorization.

Permission is given to make multiple copies of any of these resources for educational use.

Shadow and Substance Diagram

MESSIAH and the MESSIANIC HOPE

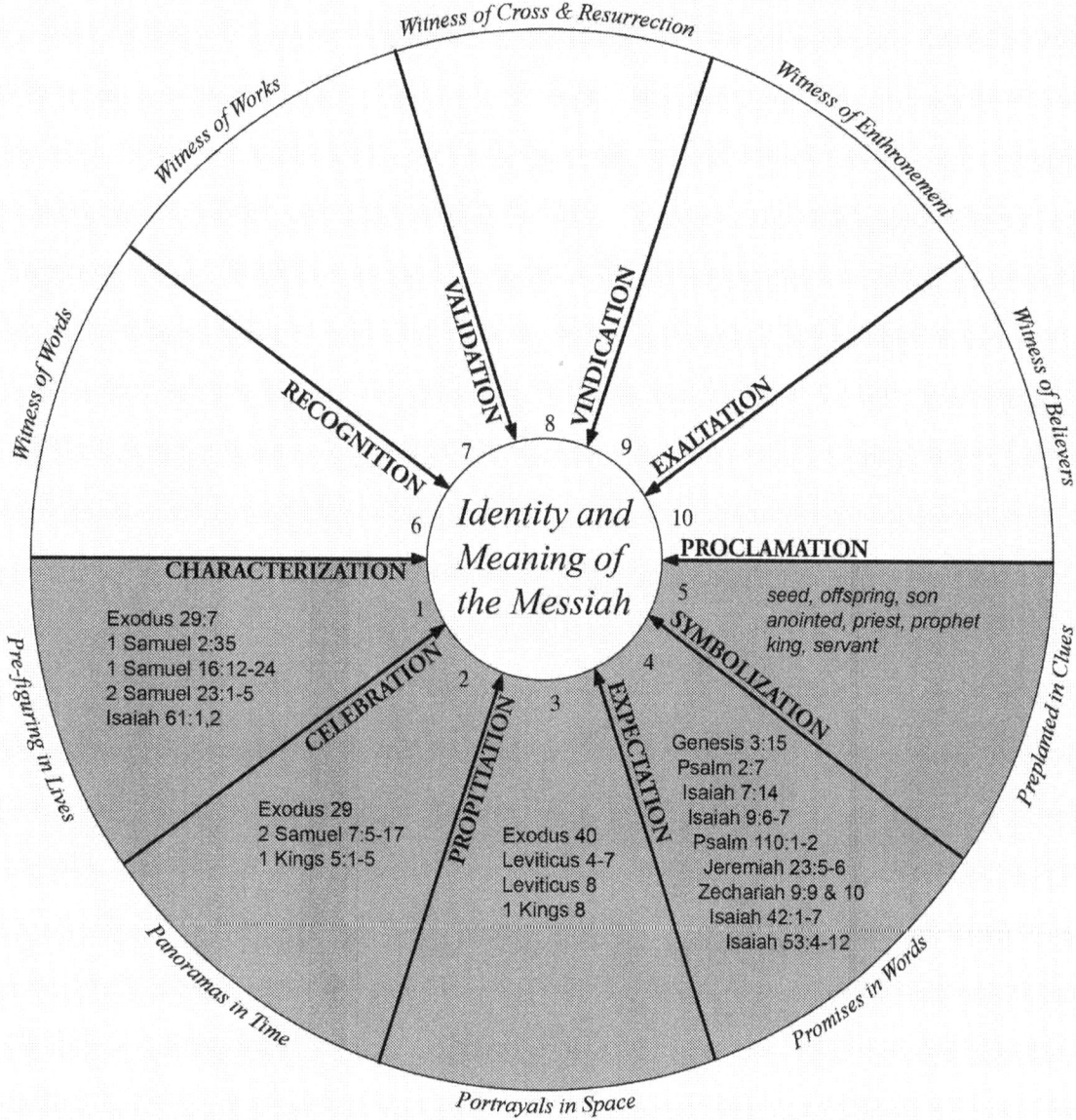

Witness of Cross & Resurrection

Witness of Works

Witness of Enthronement

Witness of Words

VALIDATION

VINDICATION

Witness of Believers

RECOGNITION

EXALTATION

7

8

9

Identity and Meaning of the Messiah

6

10

CHARACTERIZATION

PROCLAMATION

Pre-figuring in Lives

1

5

seed, offspring, son
anointed, priest, prophet
king, servant

Exodus 29:7
1 Samuel 2:35
1 Samuel 16:12-24
2 Samuel 23:1-5
Isaiah 61:1,2

CELEBRATION

2

4

SYMBOLIZATION

Preplanted in Clues

3

EXPECTATION

Exodus 29
2 Samuel 7:5-17
1 Kings 5:1-5

PROPITIATION

Exodus 40
Leviticus 4-7
Leviticus 8
1 Kings 8

Genesis 3:15
Psalm 2:7
Isaiah 7:14
Isaiah 9:6-7
Psalm 110:1-2
Jeremiah 23:5-6
Zechariah 9:9 & 10
Isaiah 42:1-7
Isaiah 53:4-12

Panoramas in Time

Promises in Words

Portrayals in Space

Shadow and Substance Diagram

MESSIAH and ADAM

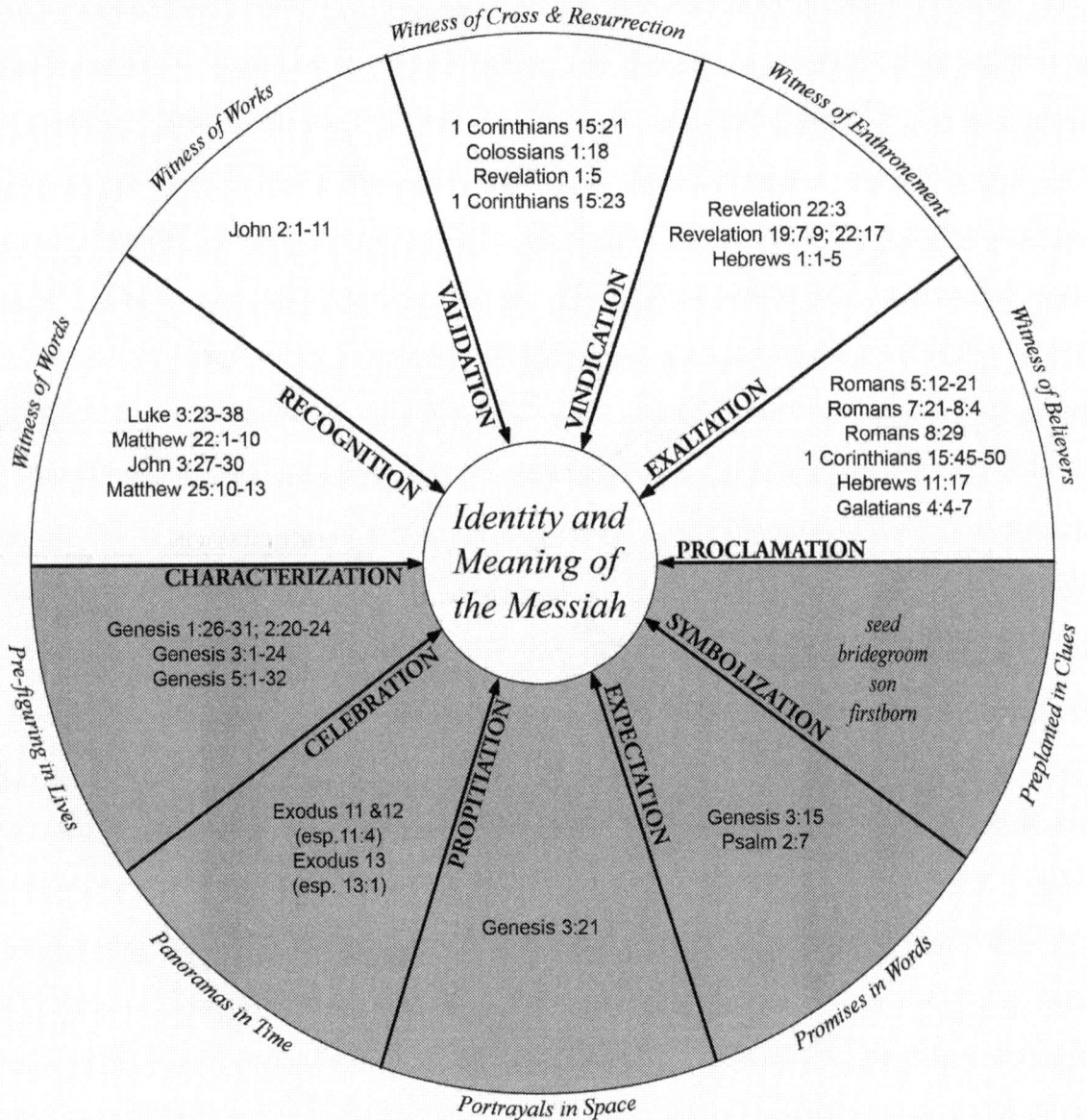

III
Shadow and Substance Diagram
MESSIAH and ABRAHAM

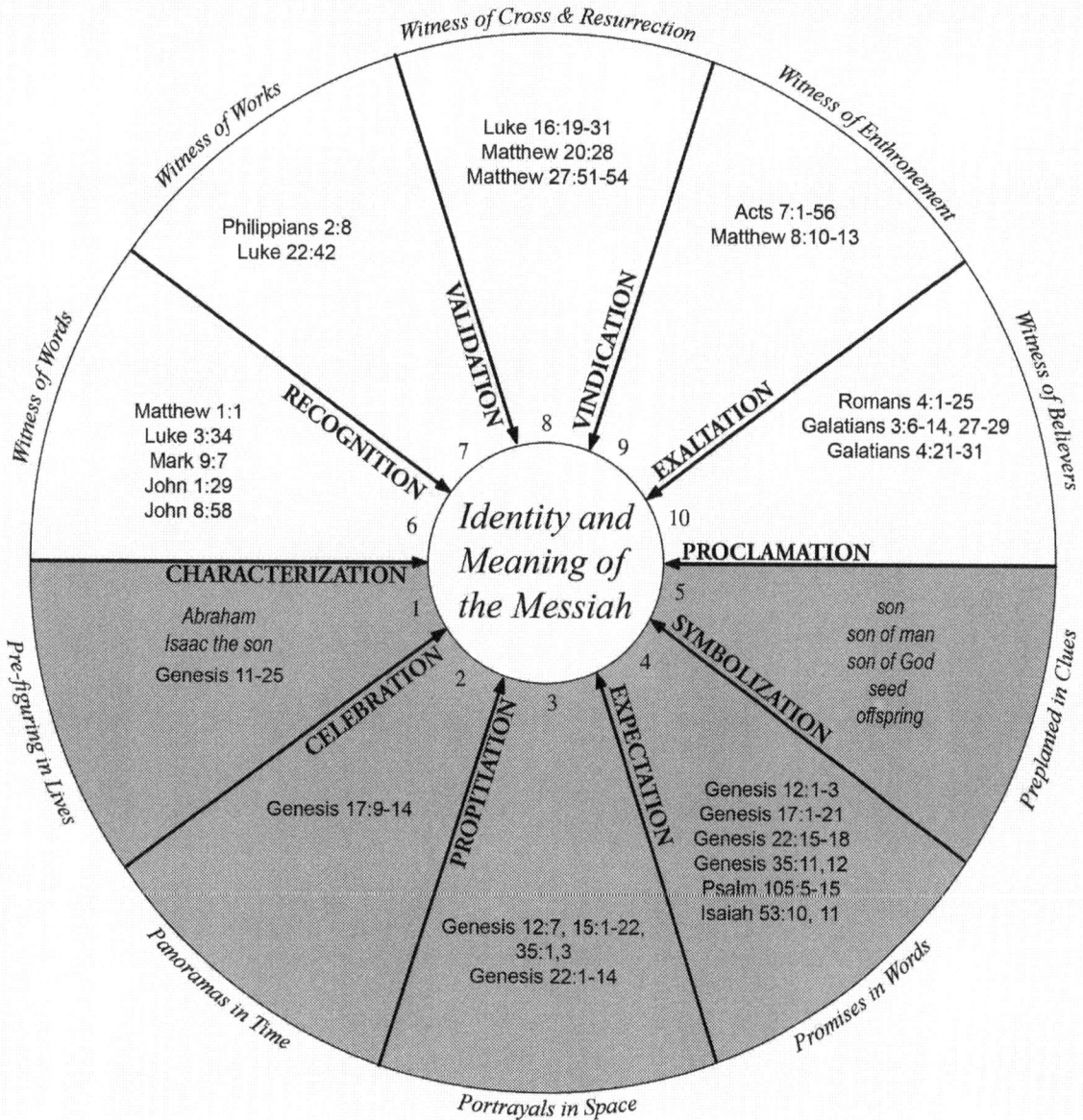

Shadow and Substance Diagram

MESSIAH and MOSES

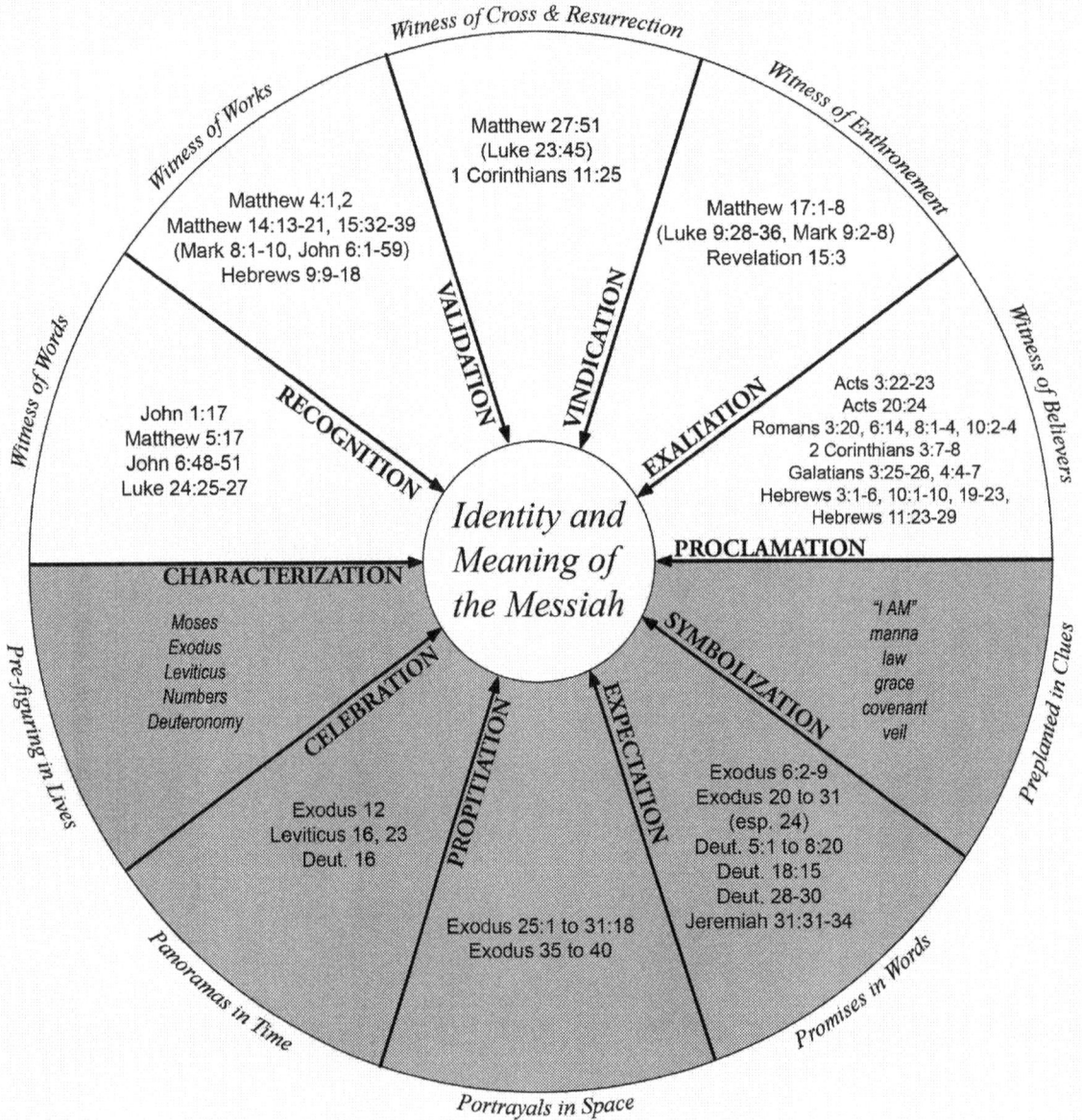

Witness of Cross & Resurrection

Witness of Works

Witness of Enthronement

Witness of Words

Witness of Believers

Matthew 27:51
(Luke 23:45)
1 Corinthians 11:25

Matthew 4:1,2
Matthew 14:13-21, 15:32-39
(Mark 8:1-10, John 6:1-59)
Hebrews 9:9-18

Matthew 17:1-8
(Luke 9:28-36, Mark 9:2-8)
Revelation 15:3

VALIDATION

VINDICATION

RECOGNITION

EXALTATION

John 1:17
Matthew 5:17
John 6:48-51
Luke 24:25-27

Acts 3:22-23
Acts 20:24
Romans 3:20, 6:14, 8:1-4, 10:2-4
2 Corinthians 3:7-8
Galatians 3:25-26, 4:4-7
Hebrews 3:1-6, 10:1-10, 19-23,
Hebrews 11:23-29

Identity and Meaning of the Messiah

CHARACTERIZATION

PROCLAMATION

Pre-figuring in Lives

Preplanted in Clues

Moses
Exodus
Leviticus
Numbers
Deuteronomy

"I AM"
manna
law
grace
covenant
veil

CELEBRATION

SYMBOLIZATION

PROPITIATION

EXPECTATION

Exodus 12
Leviticus 16, 23
Deut. 16

Exodus 6:2-9
Exodus 20 to 31
(esp. 24)
Deut. 5:1 to 8:20
Deut. 18:15
Deut. 28-30
Jeremiah 31:31-34

Exodus 25:1 to 31:18
Exodus 35 to 40

Panoramas in Time

Promises in Words

Portrayals in Space

Shadow and Substance Diagram

MESSIAH and the TABERNACLE

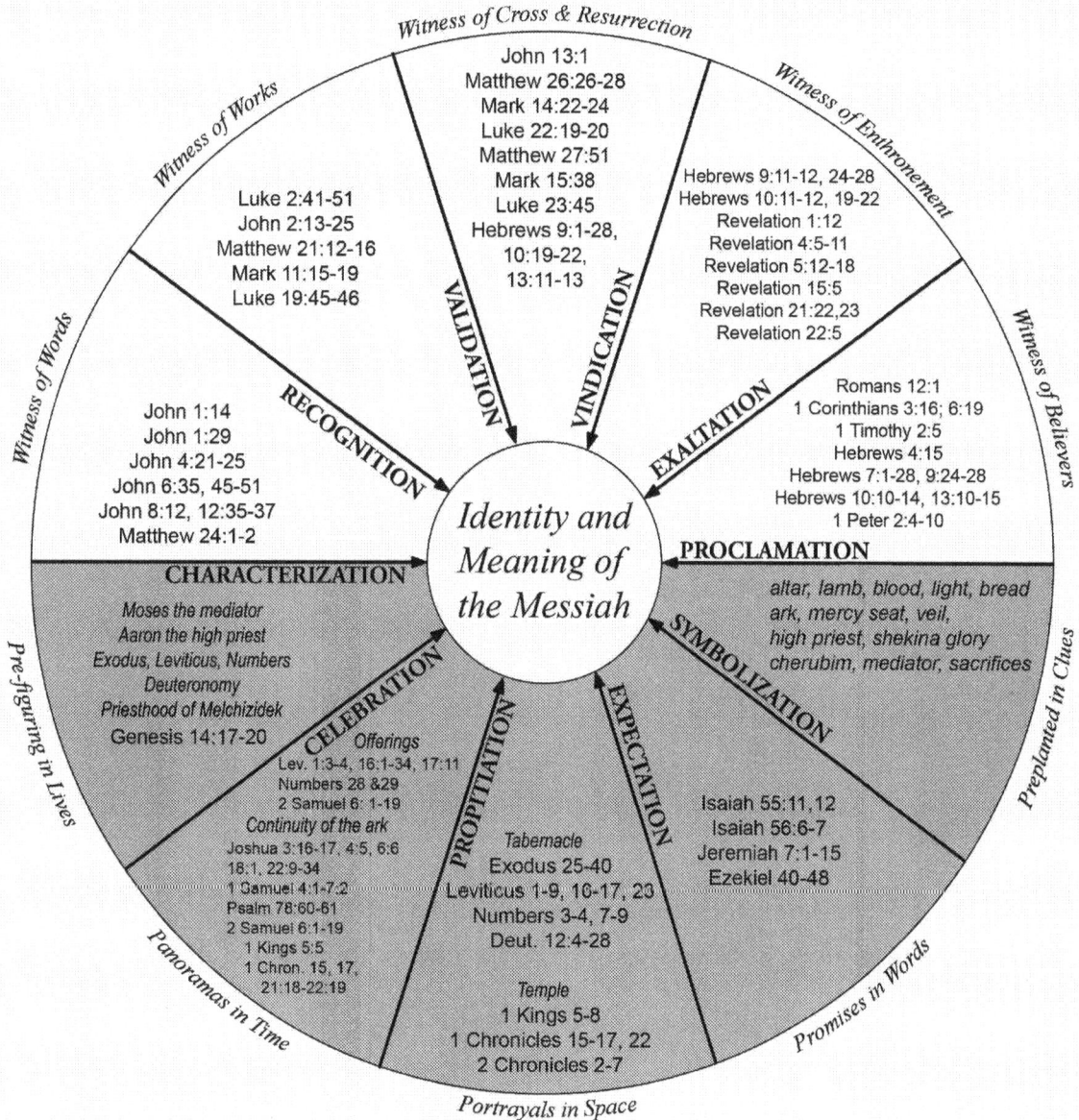

Witness of Cross & Resurrection

John 13:1
Matthew 26:26-28
Mark 14:22-24
Luke 22:19-20
Matthew 27:51
Mark 15:38
Luke 23:45
Hebrews 9:1-28,
10:19-22,
13:11-13

Witness of Works

Luke 2:41-51
John 2:13-25
Matthew 21:12-16
Mark 11:15-19
Luke 19:45-46

Witness of Enthronement

Hebrews 9:11-12, 24-28
Hebrews 10:11-12, 19-22
Revelation 1:12
Revelation 4:5-11
Revelation 5:12-18
Revelation 15:5
Revelation 21:22,23
Revelation 22:5

Witness of Words

John 1:14
John 1:29
John 4:21-25
John 6:35, 45-51
John 8:12, 12:35-37
Matthew 24:1-2

Witness of Believers

Romans 12:1
1 Corinthians 3:16; 6:19
1 Timothy 2:5
Hebrews 4:15
Hebrews 7:1-28, 9:24-28
Hebrews 10:10-14, 13:10-15
1 Peter 2:4-10

RECOGNITION **VALIDATION** **VINDICATION** **EXALTATION**

Identity and Meaning of the Messiah

CHARACTERIZATION

PROCLAMATION

Moses the mediator
Aaron the high priest
Exodus, Leviticus, Numbers
Deuteronomy
Priesthood of Melchizidek
Genesis 14:17-20

altar, lamb, blood, light, bread
ark, mercy seat, veil,
high priest, shekina glory
cherubim, mediator, sacrifices

CELEBRATION **PROPITIATION** **EXPECTATION** **SYMBOLIZATION**

Offerings
Lev. 1:3-4, 16:1-34, 17:11
Numbers 28 &29
2 Samuel 6: 1-19
Continuity of the ark
Joshua 3:16-17, 4:5, 6:6
18:1, 22:9-34
1 Samuel 4:1-7:2
Psalm 78:60-61
2 Samuel 6:1-19
1 Kings 5:5
1 Chron. 15, 17,
21:18-22:19

Tabernacle
Exodus 25-40
Leviticus 1-9, 10-17, 23
Numbers 3-4, 7-9
Deut. 12:4-28

Temple
1 Kings 5-8
1 Chronicles 15-17, 22
2 Chronicles 2-7

Isaiah 55:11,12
Isaiah 56:6-7
Jeremiah 7:1-15
Ezekiel 40-48

Pre-figuring in Lives

Panoramas in Time

Portrayals in Space

Promises in Words

Preplanted in Clues

Shadow and Substance Diagram
MESSIAH and the FEASTS

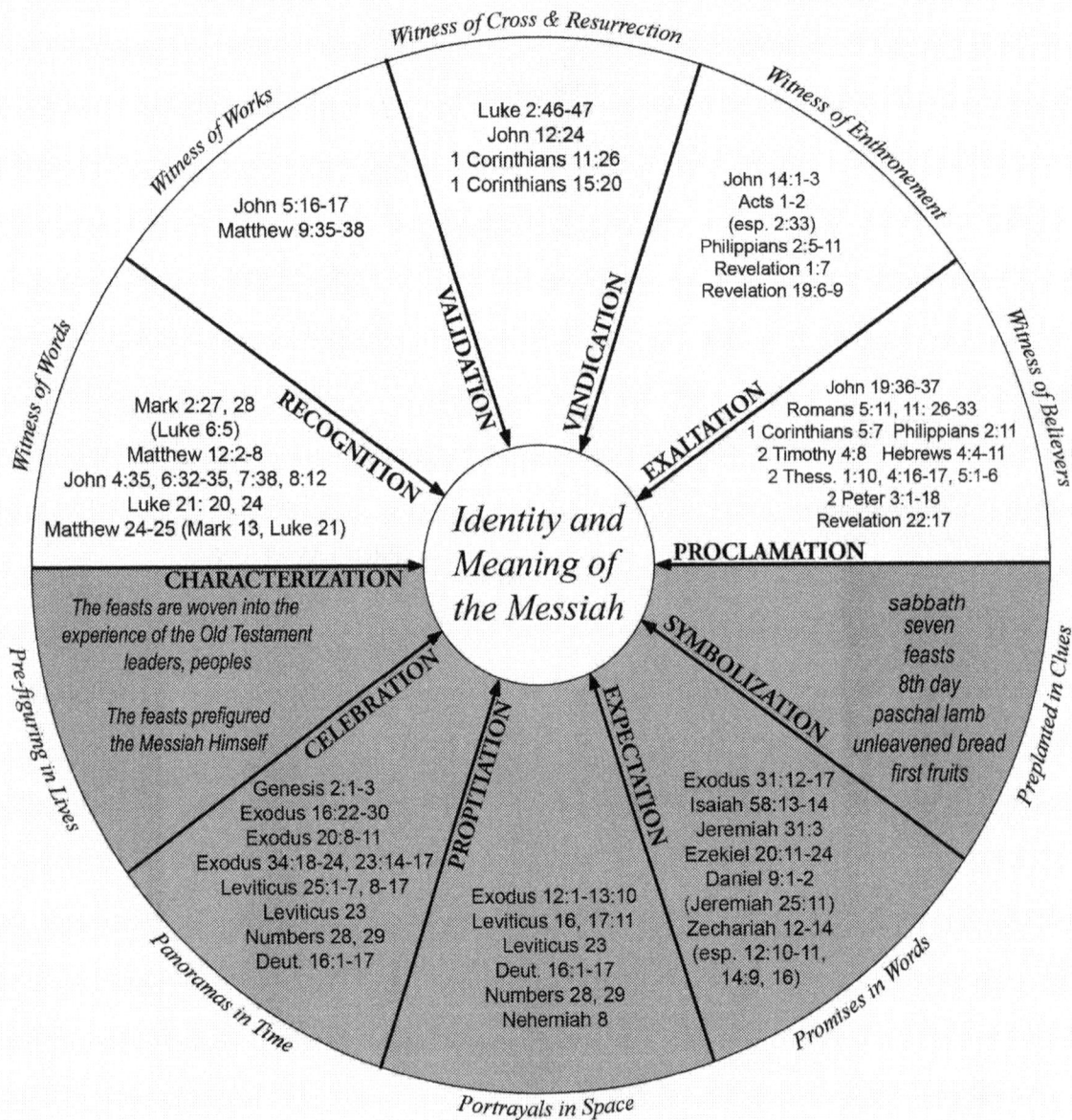

Witness of Cross & Resurrection

Witness of Works

Witness of Enthronement

Luke 2:46-47
John 12:24
1 Corinthians 11:26
1 Corinthians 15:20

John 5:16-17
Matthew 9:35-38

John 14:1-3
Acts 1-2
(esp. 2:33)
Philippians 2:5-11
Revelation 1:7
Revelation 19:6-9

VALIDATION

VINDICATION

Witness of Words

Witness of Believers

Mark 2:27, 28
(Luke 6:5)
Matthew 12:2-8
John 4:35, 6:32-35, 7:38, 8:12
Luke 21: 20, 24
Matthew 24-25 (Mark 13, Luke 21)

RECOGNITION

EXALTATION

John 19:36-37
Romans 5:11, 11: 26-33
1 Corinthians 5:7   Philippians 2:11
2 Timothy 4:8   Hebrews 4:4-11
2 Thess. 1:10, 4:16-17, 5:1-6
2 Peter 3:1-18
Revelation 22:17

Identity and Meaning of the Messiah

CHARACTERIZATION

PROCLAMATION

The feasts are woven into the
experience of the Old Testament
leaders, peoples

The feasts prefigured
the Messiah Himself

CELEBRATION

SYMBOLIZATION

sabbath
seven
feasts
8th day
paschal lamb
unleavened bread
first fruits

Pre-figuring in Lives

Preplanted in Clues

Genesis 2:1-3
Exodus 16:22-30
Exodus 20:8-11
Exodus 34:18-24, 23:14-17
Leviticus 25:1-7, 8-17
Leviticus 23
Numbers 28, 29
Deut. 16:1-17

PROPITIATION

EXPECTATION

Exodus 31:12-17
Isaiah 58:13-14
Jeremiah 31:3
Ezekiel 20:11-24
Daniel 9:1-2
(Jeremiah 25:11)
Zechariah 12-14
(esp. 12:10-11,
14:9, 16)

Exodus 12:1-13:10
Leviticus 16, 17:11
Leviticus 23
Deut. 16:1-17
Numbers 28, 29
Nehemiah 8

Panoramas in Time

Promises in Words

Portrayals in Space

Shadow and Substance Diagram

MESSIAH and DAVID

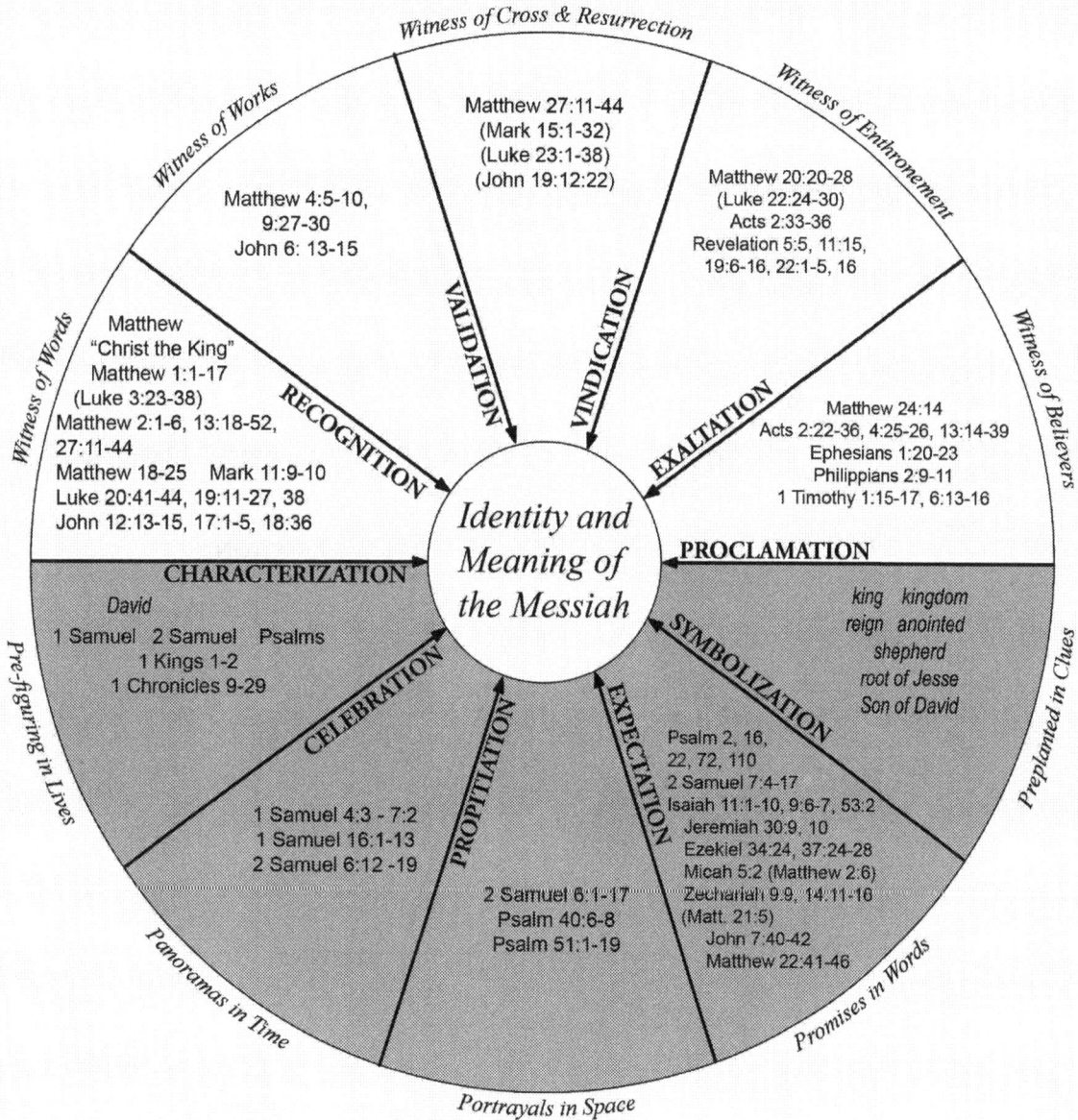

Shadow and Substance Diagram

MESSIAH and the PROPHETS, PROPHECIES

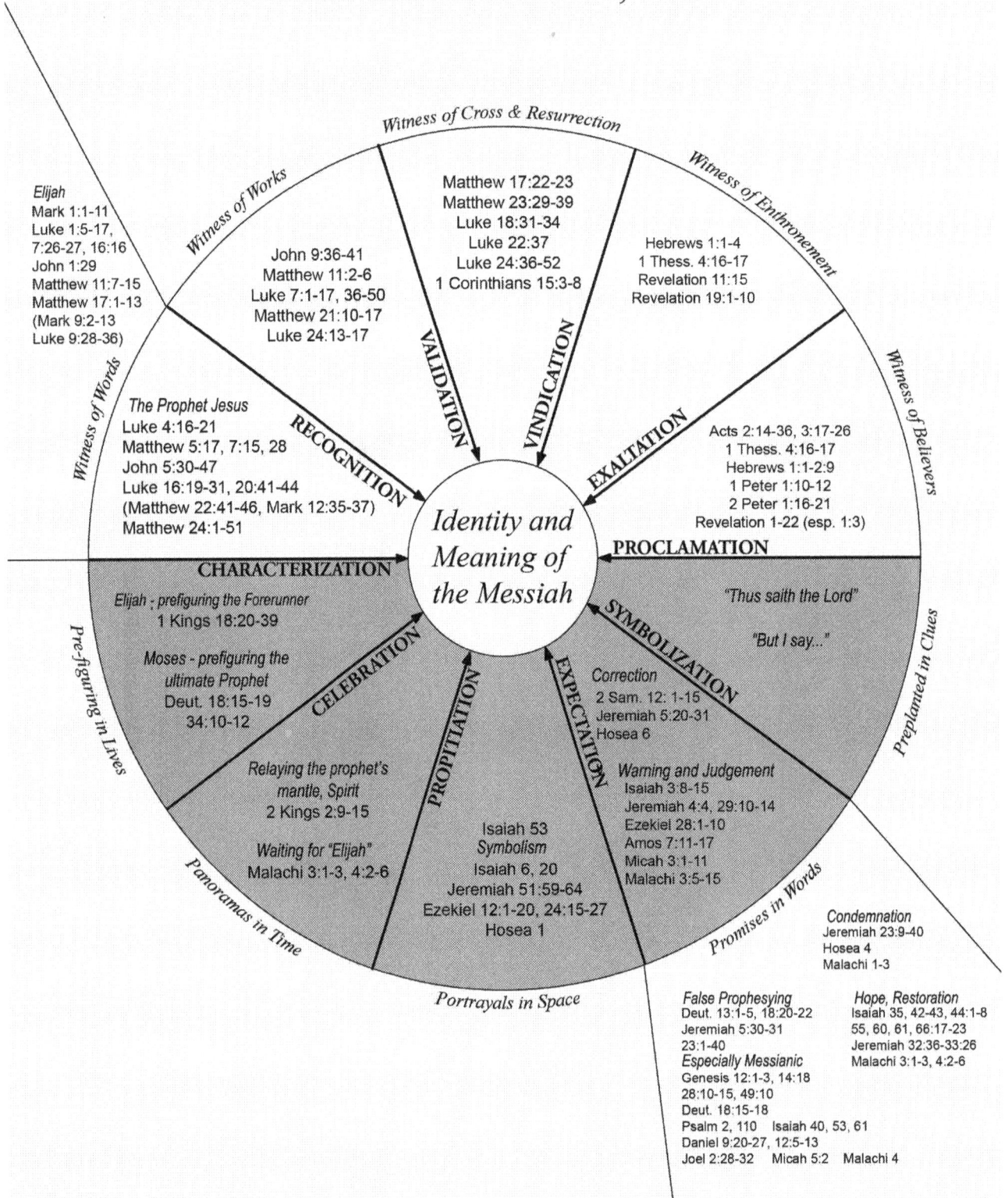

Witness of Cross & Resurrection

Witness of Works

Witness of Enthronement

Elijah
Mark 1:1-11
Luke 1:5-17,
7:26-27, 16:16
John 1:29
Matthew 11:7-15
Matthew 17:1-13
(Mark 9:2-13
Luke 9:28-36)

Matthew 17:22-23
Matthew 23:29-39
Luke 18:31-34
Luke 22:37
Luke 24:36-52
1 Corinthians 15:3-8

John 9:36-41
Matthew 11:2-6
Luke 7:1-17, 36-50
Matthew 21:10-17
Luke 24:13-17

Hebrews 1:1-4
1 Thess. 4:16-17
Revelation 11:15
Revelation 19:1-10

Witness of Words

VALIDATION

VINDICATION

Witness of Believers

The Prophet Jesus
Luke 4:16-21
Matthew 5:17, 7:15, 28
John 5:30-47
Luke 16:19-31, 20:41-44
(Matthew 22:41-46, Mark 12:35-37)
Matthew 24:1-51

RECOGNITION

EXALTATION

Acts 2:14-36, 3:17-26
1 Thess. 4:16-17
Hebrews 1:1-2:9
1 Peter 1:10-12
2 Peter 1:16-21
Revelation 1-22 (esp. 1:3)

CHARACTERIZATION

Identity and Meaning of the Messiah

PROCLAMATION

Elijah - prefiguring the Forerunner
1 Kings 18:20-39

"Thus saith the Lord"

"But I say..."

Pre-figuring in Lives

Moses - prefiguring the
ultimate Prophet
Deut. 18:15-19
34:10-12

CELEBRATION

PROPITIATION

EXPECTATION

SYMBOLIZATION

Correction
2 Sam. 12: 1-15
Jeremiah 5:20-31
Hosea 6

Preplanted in Clues

Relaying the prophet's
mantle, Spirit
2 Kings 2:9-15

Warning and Judgement
Isaiah 3:8-15
Jeremiah 4:4, 29:10-14
Ezekiel 28:1-10
Amos 7:11-17
Micah 3:1-11
Malachi 3:5-15

Waiting for "Elijah"
Malachi 3:1-3, 4:2-6

Isaiah 53
Symbolism
Isaiah 6, 20
Jeremiah 51:59-64
Ezekiel 12:1-20, 24:15-27
Hosea 1

Panoramas in Time

Promises in Words

Condemnation
Jeremiah 23:9-40
Hosea 4
Malachi 1-3

Portrayals in Space

False Prophesying
Deut. 13:1-5, 18:20-22
Jeremiah 5:30-31
23:1-40
Especially Messianic
Genesis 12:1-3, 14:18
28:10-15, 49:10
Deut. 18:15-18
Psalm 2, 110   Isaiah 40, 53, 61
Daniel 9:20-27, 12:5-13
Joel 2:28-32   Micah 5:2   Malachi 4

Hope, Restoration
Isaiah 35, 42-43, 44:1-8
55, 60, 61, 66:17-23
Jeremiah 32:36-33:26
Malachi 3:1-3, 4:2-6

Shadow and Substance Diagram

The MESSIAH MANIFESTED

*(For Scripture references, refer back to circle diagrams of the particular chapters
noted in the sections below with Roman numerals)*

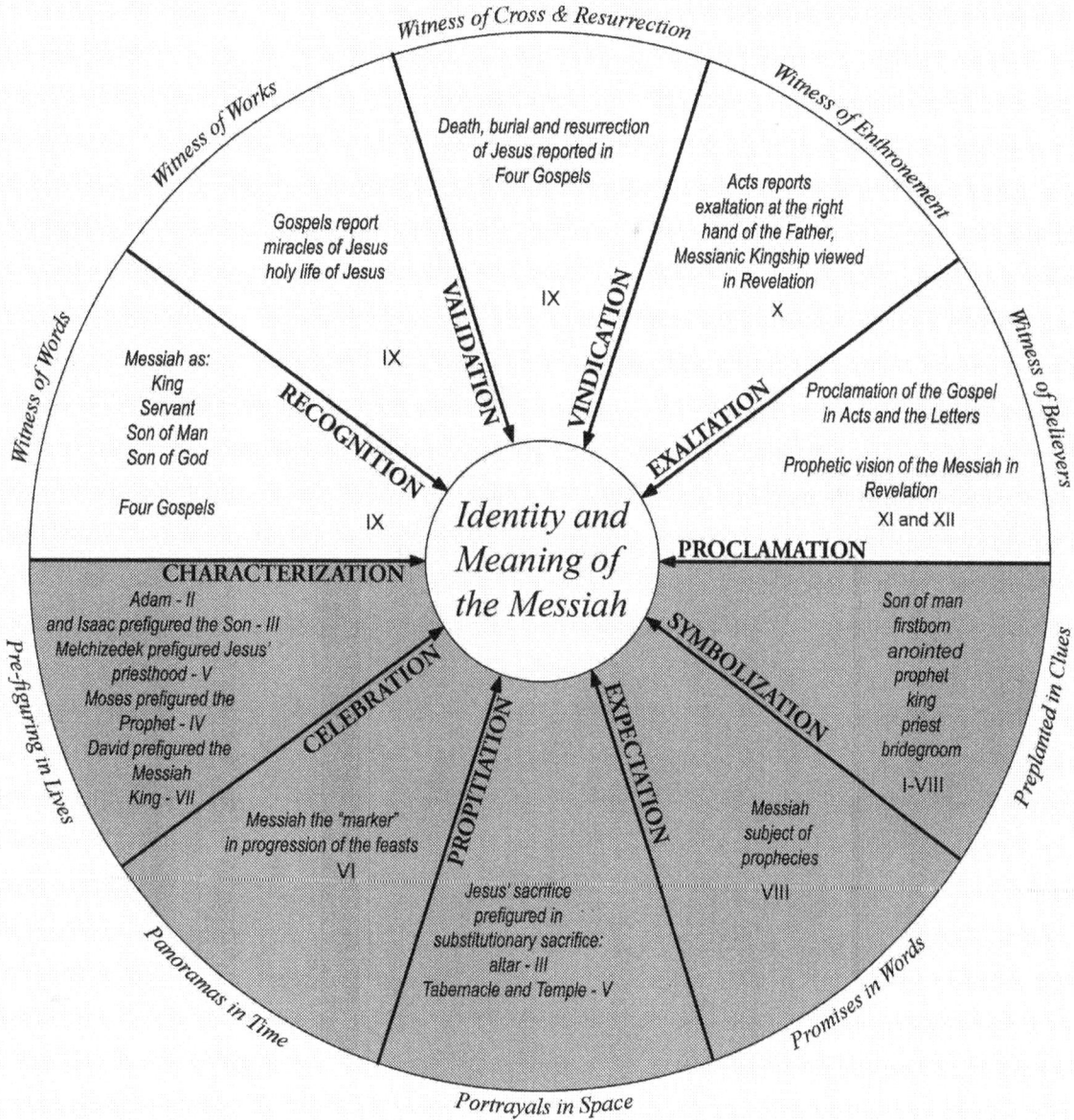

Identity and Meaning of the Messiah

Witness of Cross & Resurrection

Witness of Works

Witness of Enthronement

Witness of Words

Witness of Believers

Pre-figuring in Lives

Preplanted in Clues

Panoramas in Time

Promises in Words

Portrayals in Space

VALIDATION — IX

VINDICATION — IX

RECOGNITION — IX

EXALTATION — X

CHARACTERIZATION

PROCLAMATION

CELEBRATION

SYMBOLIZATION

PROPITIATION

EXPECTATION

Death, burial and resurrection of Jesus reported in Four Gospels

Gospels report miracles of Jesus holy life of Jesus

Acts reports exaltation at the right hand of the Father, Messianic Kingship viewed in Revelation — X

Messiah as:
King
Servant
Son of Man
Son of God

Four Gospels — IX

Proclamation of the Gospel in Acts and the Letters

Prophetic vision of the Messiah in Revelation — XI and XII

Adam - II
and Isaac prefigured the Son - III
Melchizedek prefigured Jesus' priesthood - V
Moses prefigured the Prophet - IV
David prefigured the Messiah King - VII

Son of man
firstborn
anointed
prophet
king
priest
bridegroom — I-VIII

Messiah the "marker" in progression of the feasts — VI

Jesus' sacrifice prefigured in substitutionary sacrifice:
altar - III
Tabernacle and Temple - V

Messiah subject of prophecies — VIII

Shadow and Substance Diagram

MESSIAH and the HOLY SPIRIT

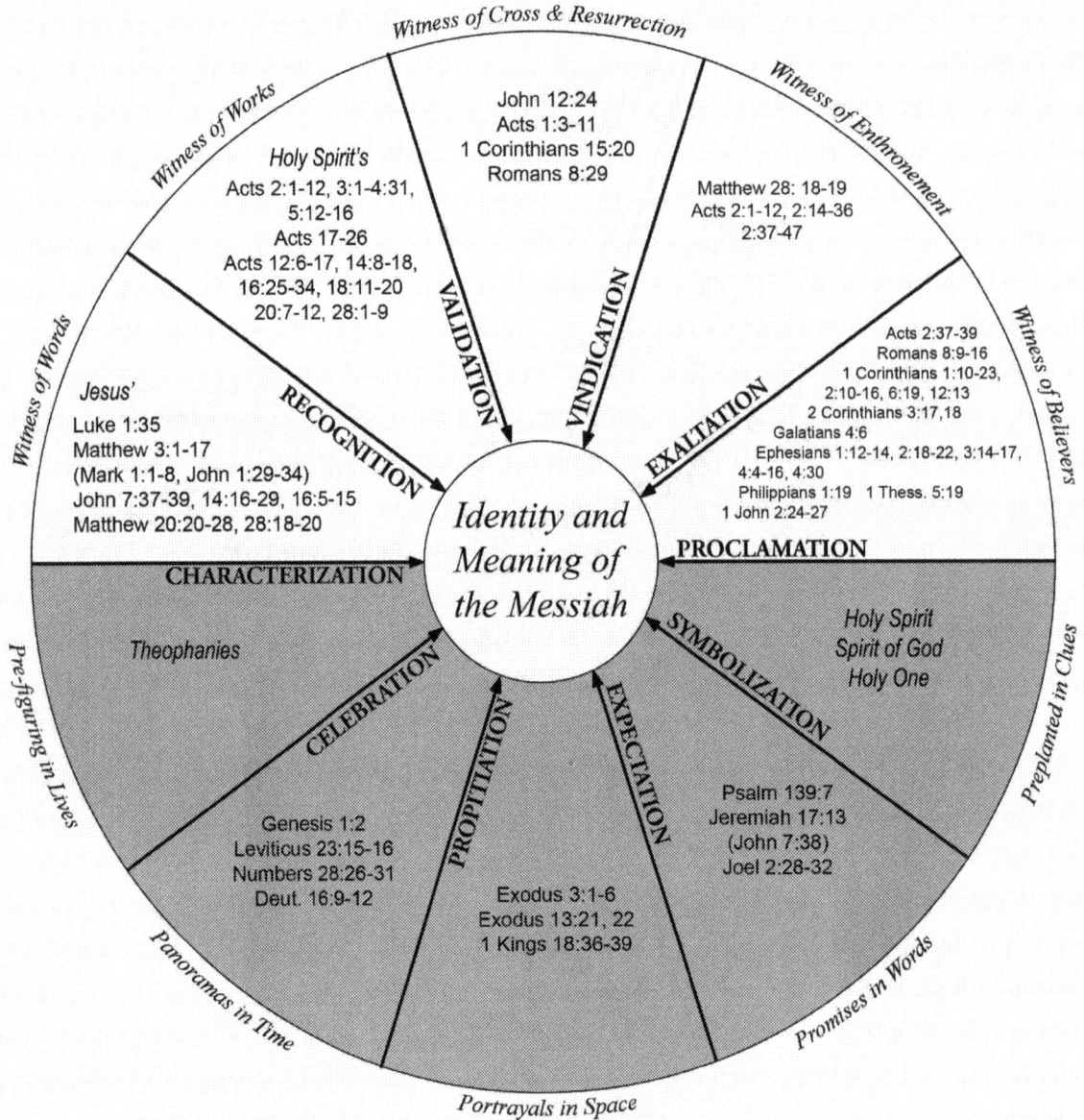

Witness of Cross & Resurrection

Witness of Works

Witness of Enthronement

Holy Spirit's
Acts 2:1-12, 3:1-4:31,
5:12-16
Acts 17-26
Acts 12:6-17, 14:8-18,
16:25-34, 18:11-20
20:7-12, 28:1-9

John 12:24
Acts 1:3-11
1 Corinthians 15:20
Romans 8:29

Matthew 28: 18-19
Acts 2:1-12, 2:14-36
2:37-47

Witness of Words

Witness of Believers

VALIDATION

VINDICATION

Jesus'
Luke 1:35
Matthew 3:1-17
(Mark 1:1-8, John 1:29-34)
John 7:37-39, 14:16-29, 16:5-15
Matthew 20:20-28, 28:18-20

RECOGNITION

EXALTATION

Acts 2:37-39
Romans 8:9-16
1 Corinthians 1:10-23,
2:10-16, 6:19, 12:13
2 Corinthians 3:17,18
Galatians 4:6
Ephesians 1:12-14, 2:18-22, 3:14-17,
4:4-16, 4:30
Philippians 1:19   1 Thess. 5:19
1 John 2:24-27

Identity and Meaning of the Messiah

CHARACTERIZATION

PROCLAMATION

Theophanies

Holy Spirit
Spirit of God
Holy One

Pre-figuring in Lives

CELEBRATION

SYMBOLIZATION

Preplanted in Clues

PROPITIATION

EXPECTATION

Genesis 1:2
Leviticus 23:15-16
Numbers 28:26-31
Deut. 16:9-12

Psalm 139:7
Jeremiah 17:13
(John 7:38)
Joel 2:28-32

Exodus 3:1-6
Exodus 13:21, 22
1 Kings 18:36-39

Panoramas in Time

Promises in Words

Portrayals in Space

Shadow and Substance Diagram
The MESSIAH'S COMMITY

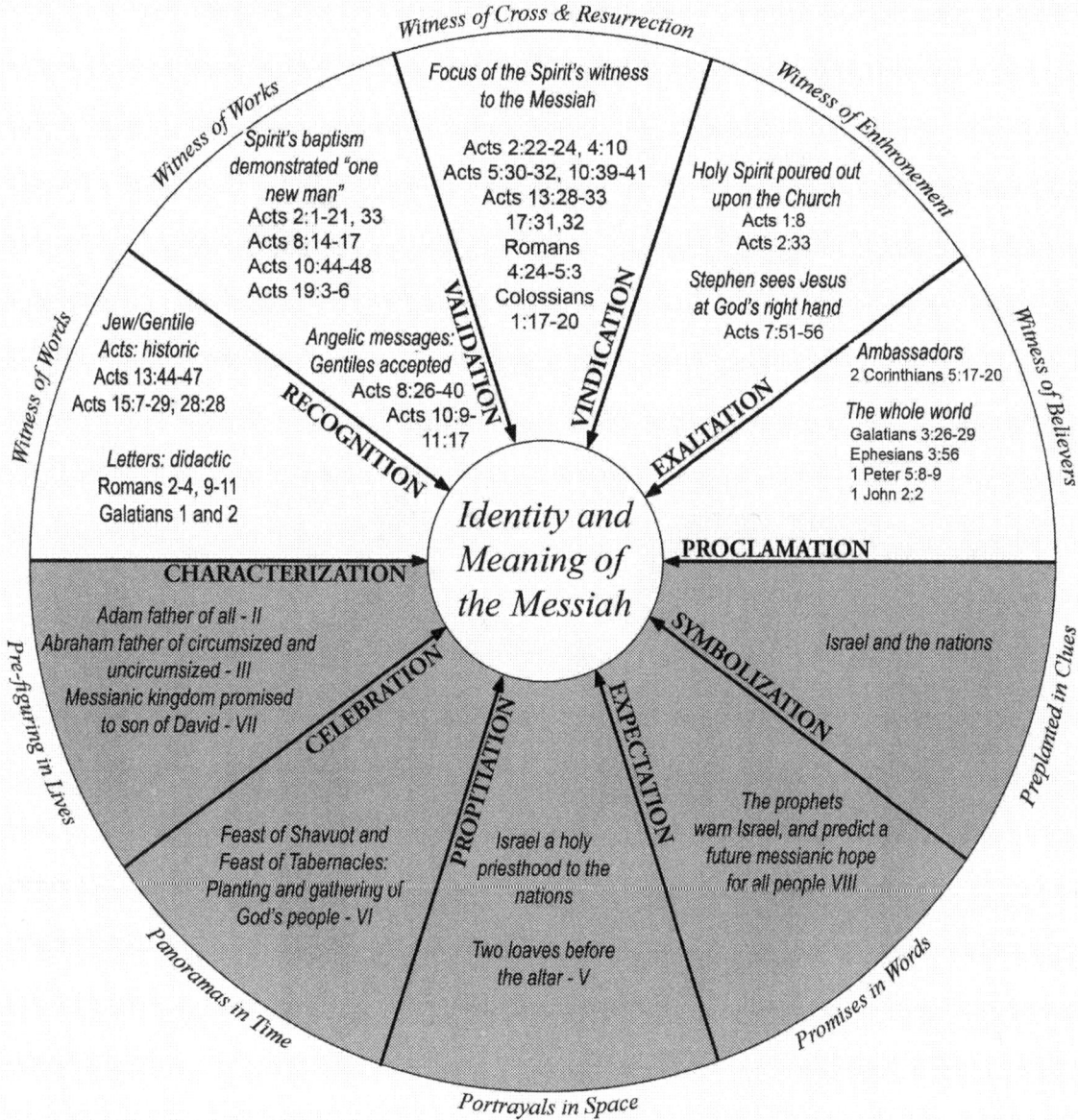

Witness of Cross & Resurrection

Witness of Works

Witness of Enthronement

Focus of the Spirit's witness
to the Messiah

Acts 2:22-24, 4:10
Acts 5:30-32, 10:39-41
Acts 13:28-33
17:31,32
Romans
4:24-5:3
Colossians
1:17-20

Spirit's baptism
demonstrated "one
new man"
Acts 2:1-21, 33
Acts 8:14-17
Acts 10:44-48
Acts 19:3-6

Holy Spirit poured out
upon the Church
Acts 1:8
Acts 2:33

Stephen sees Jesus
at God's right hand
Acts 7:51-56

Witness of Words

Jew/Gentile
Acts: historic
Acts 13:44-47
Acts 15:7-29; 28:28

Letters: didactic
Romans 2-4, 9-11
Galatians 1 and 2

Angelic messages:
Gentiles accepted
Acts 8:26-40
Acts 10:9-
11:17

VALIDATION

VINDICATION

Ambassadors
2 Corinthians 5:17-20

The whole world
Galatians 3:26-29
Ephesians 3:56
1 Peter 5:8-9
1 John 2:2

Witness of Believers

RECOGNITION

EXALTATION

*Identity and
Meaning of
the Messiah*

PROCLAMATION

CHARACTERIZATION

Adam father of all - II
Abraham father of circumsized and
uncircumsized - III
Messianic kingdom promised
to son of David - VII

SYMBOLIZATION

Israel and the nations

Pre-figuring in Lives

CELEBRATION

PROPITIATION

EXPECTATION

Preplanted in Clues

Feast of Shavuot and
Feast of Tabernacles:
Planting and gathering of
God's people - VI

Israel a holy
priesthood to the
nations

Two loaves before
the altar - V

The prophets
warn Israel, and predict a
future messianic hope
for all people VIII

Panoramas in Time

Portrayals in Space

Promises in Words

Shadow and Substance Diagram

MESSIAH'S CONSUMMATION

(For scripture references, refer back to circle diagrams of the Messiah Mystery sections noted with Roman numerals.)

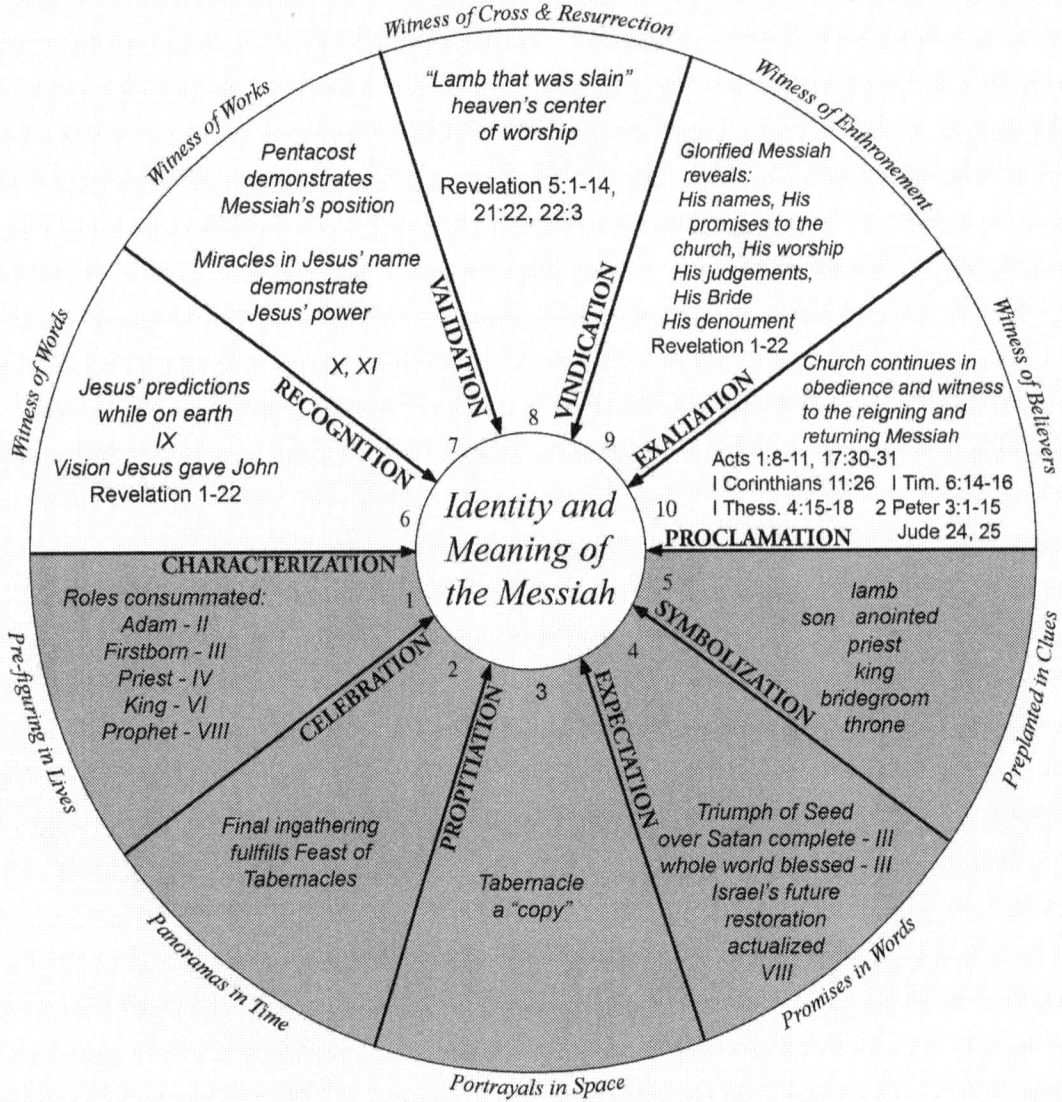

Witness of Cross & Resurrection

Witness of Works

Witness of Enthronement

Witness of Words

Witness of Believers

"Lamb that was slain" heaven's center of worship

Revelation 5:1-14, 21:22, 22:3

Pentacost demonstrates Messiah's position

Miracles in Jesus' name demonstrate Jesus' power

X, XI

Glorified Messiah reveals:
His names, His promises to the church, His worship
His judgements,
His Bride
His denoument
Revelation 1-22

VALIDATION

VINDICATION

RECOGNITION

Jesus' predictions while on earth
IX
Vision Jesus gave John
Revelation 1-22

EXALTATION

Church continues in obedience and witness to the reigning and returning Messiah
Acts 1:8-11, 17:30-31
I Corinthians 11:26   I Tim. 6:14-16
I Thess. 4:15-18   2 Peter 3:1-15
Jude 24, 25

Identity and Meaning of the Messiah

PROCLAMATION

CHARACTERIZATION

Roles consummated:
Adam - II
Firstborn - III
Priest - IV
King - VI
Prophet - VIII

SYMBOLIZATION

lamb
son   anointed
priest
king
bridegroom
throne

CELEBRATION

PROPITIATION

EXPECTATION

Pre-figuring in Lives

Final ingathering fullfills Feast of Tabernacles

Tabernacle a "copy"

Triumph of Seed over Satan complete - III
whole world blessed - III
Israel's future restoration actualized
VIII

Preplanted in Clues

Panoramas in Time

Promises in Words

Portrayals in Space

6   1   2   3   4   5   7   8   9   10

TEMPLATE:

SHADOW AND SUBSTANCE CIRCLE RESPONSES

Section:
Name:
Date:

OLD TESTAMENT lower "shadow" half notations:
Section 1: Characterization

Section 2: Celebration

Section 3: Propitiation

Section 4: Expectation

Section 5: Symbolization

NEW TESTAMENT upper "substance" half notations:
Section 6: Recognition

Section 7: Validation

Section 8: Vindication

Section 9: Exaltation

Section 10: Proclamation

Permission is given to copy for educational use.

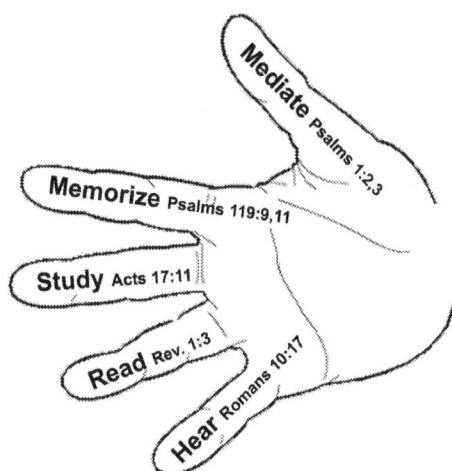

THE GOLDEN KEY OF MEMORIZATION

The S and S Circles collect many scriptures related to each section, and the blank study template suggests you add your own. However, in the final analysis, simplification is often a wise rule. The Navigators' Topical Memory System, for instance, helps many Christians to conserve their study and quickly locate it to pass it on as the Spirit of God gives opportunity. Memorizing scripture is a basic way to be "ready to give an answer for the hope that is in you."

Furthermore, especially for adults, memorizing key scriptures helps us recall the passage in which the verses are imbedded. They become the horizontal rack on which various conceptual hats can be hung. The Navigators' TMS is properly called the "Topical Memory System," because the verses chosen cover a wide range of subjects in which believers need to be well "versed" literally.

Pictured above is the Navigator's HAND graphic. It's a simple but clear visual aid. Trying to grasp a Bible with the fifth finger shows the 5th (hearing) to be the weakest for holding onto the word of God. The 4th finger (reading) is obviously the next weakest, the 3rd (studying) gets a stronger hold, the 2nd (memorizing) gets a good grasp, when combined with the thumb (meditating). Scripture memory is sometimes relegated to teaching children. Children are quite able to sing back a verse without understanding it. Adults, however, usually must understand a verse to memorize it in a way that sticks. (Repetition, of course, is necessary – daily for a month, usually, for getting a permanent hold on God's precious words.) It is helpful, when memorizing a verse, to make a thoughtful study of the paragraph in which it appears, at the same time. Thus the verse becomes the key for opening up the topic of the passage, and a door opening into God's presence.

The following verses (NIV) are key scriptures that match the twelve sections of the Messiah Mystery topics, plus three others that are deeply related to the study. They can be copied in sheets or turned into a card packet. Disciplined study of God's word can become one of the most significant investments in a believer's life. A Navigator friend put it this way, "It's all very nice to own a telephone book, but you really do need to have 911 memorized!"

* The Hand diagram is used by permission of the Navigators, copyright 1979. All rights reserved.

* This page, and the accompanying verses, may be copied for educational purposes.

I. Introducing the Messiah

In the beginning was the Word, and the Word was with God, and the Word was God. ...The Word became flesh and made his dwelling among us. We have seen his glory, the glory of the One and Only, who came from the Father, full of grace and truth.

John 1:1, 14

II. The Messiah and Adam

For since death came through a man, the resurrection of the dead comes also through a man. For as in Adam all die, so in Christ all will be made alive.

1 Corinthians 15:21,22

III. The Messiah and Abraham

By faith Abraham, when God tested him, offered Isaac as a sacrifice. He who had received the promises was about to sacrifice his one and only son, even though God had said to him, "It is through Isaac that your offspring will be reckoned." Abraham reasoned that God could raise the dead, and figuratively speaking, he did receive Isaac back from death.

Hebrews 11:17-19

IV. The Messiah and Moses

For this reason Christ is the mediator of a new covenant, that those who are called may receive the promised eternal inheritance - now that he has died as a ransom to set them free from the sins committed under the first covenant.

Hebrews 9:15

V. The Messiah and the Tabernacle

It was necessary, then, for the copies of the heavenly things to be purified with these sacrifices, but the heavenly things themselves with better sacrifices than these. For Christ did not enter a man-made sanctuary that was only a copy of the true one; he entered heaven itself, now to appear for us in God's presence.

Hebrews 9:23,24

VI. The Messiah and the Feasts

Get rid of the old yeast that you may be a new batch without yeast - as you really are. For Christ, our Passover lamb, has been sacrificed. Therefore let us keep the Festival, not with the old yeast, the yeast of malice and wickedness, but with bread without yeast, the bread of sincerity and truth.

1 Corinthians 5:7,8

VII. The Messiah and David

"I, Jesus, have sent my angel to give you this testimony for the churches. I am the Root and the Offspring of David, and the bright Morning Star."

Revelation 22:16

VIII. The Messiah and the Prophets

He said to them, "How foolish you are, and how slow of heart to believe all that the prophets have spoken! Did not the Christ have to suffer these things and then enter his glory? And beginning with Moses and all the Prophets, he explained to them what was said in all the Scriptures concerning himself.

Luke 24:25-27

IX. The Messiah Manifested

For God so loved the world that he gave his one and only Son, that whoever believes in him shall not perish but have eternal life. For God did not send his Son into the world to condemn the world, but to save the world through him.

John 3:16-17

X. The Messiah's Gift: The Holy Spirit

Exalted to the right hand of God, he has received from the Father the promised Holy Spirit and has poured out what you now see and hear.

Acts 2:33

XI. The Messiah's Community

Consequently, you are no longer foreigners and aliens, but fellow citizens with God's people and members of God's household, built on the foundation of the apostles and prophets, with Christ Jesus himself as the chief cornerstone. In him the whole building is joined together and rises to become a holy temple in the Lord. And in him you too are being built together to become a dwelling in which God lives by his Spirit.

Ephesians 2:19-22

XII. The Messianic Consummation

Let us rejoice and be glad and give him glory! For the wedding of the Lamb has come, and his bride has made herself ready.

The Spirit and the bride say, "Come!" And let him who hears say, "Come!"

Revelation 19:7,22,17a

Shadow and Substance

These are only a shadow of what is to come; but the substance belongs to Christ RSV

These are a shadow of the things that were to come; the reality however, is found in Christ. NIV

Colossians 2:17

The Eternal Purpose

In him we have redemption through his blood, the forgiveness of sins, in accordance with the riches of God's grace that he lavished on us with all wisdom and understanding. And he made known to us the mystery of his will according to his good pleasure, which he purposed in Christ, to be put into effect when the times will have reached their fullfillment - to bring all things heaven and on earth together under one head, even Christ.

Ephesians 1:7-10

The Disciple's Charge

This grace was given us in Christ Jesus before the beginning of time, but it has now been revealed through the appearing of our Savior, Christ Jesus, who has destroyed death and has brought life and immortality to light through the gospel... What you heard from me, keep as a pattern of sound teaching, with faith and love in Christ Jesus. Guard the good deposit that was entrusted to you - guard it with the help of the Holy Spirit who lives in us.

II Timothy 1:9b-10, 13, 14

ALTERNATIVE B.

GROUP TEXTBOOK AND CHAPTER DISCUSSION

"The Messiah Mystery" is a panoramic overview of the whole Bible and therefore will take considerable time to digest. The textbook includes Assimilation and Discussion Questions at the end of each chapter, designed as a catalyst for discussion. Study partners or a larger group can use this simple, self-contained mode of study and sharing.

USES OF THE TEXT

1. "The Messiah Mystery" text can be a basis of personal study at one's own speed.

2. Familiarity with the text is a preparation for teaching in any of the modes described in the KEYS.

3. The text can be the basis of a partner or group study, either by simply going over the text together or using the Assimilation and Discussion Questions as a basis for sharing.

4. "The Messiah Mystery" can be shared with people who may be looking for a panoramic overview of the scriptures centered on Jesus the Messiah, who is found throughout the Old and New Testaments.

Procedure: In this type of class, the leader's role can be more as a facilitator or guide than as a "teacher." Study partners or a small group may find this mode allows for stimulating exchange of ideas and enjoyable fellowship with a few fellow travelers. Participants must really read the text to make this discussion mode productive. The guide is like a host to the group, welcoming and including all, and then encouraging full participation.

Timing: Moving the study fast and meeting for 1½ hours once a week, it may take months to span Genesis to Revelation. Moving slowly, it may take over a year. The KEYS include the discussion questions from the book, printed on pages 45-68.

Tips for the Guide:
1. A few ground rules stated at the initial meeting are helpful, such as the avoidance of long discussion on theological questions that have dogged the church for centuries (i.e. baptism, communion, tongues etc.)
2. Keeping an agreed-upon time frame is important.

3. The group need not slavishly discuss every question listed. To kick off the discussion, the guide might ask, *"What most impressed you about this chapter? What was your thinking in response to the first question? Someone else's response?"*

4. The closing questions "FOR PERSONAL MEDITATION" are meant to be private, not for group discussion, unless spontaneously volunteered.

5. The leader can pray for the Spirit's leading, sensing what is most vital for the group to emphasize, clarify, or discuss.

6. Prayer can be a key to a group's benefit and bonding. <u>Prayer: Conversing with God</u> by Rosalyn Rinker, suggests a helpful group-offered prayer format. It promotes an attitude that can be freeing, both to people not used to prayer, and people who expect it to be "individually performed" in turn "around the circle" – terrifying to newcomers! Conversational prayer puts the burden of voiced prayer on the Holy Spirit, who will move some in the group to add their sentence, phrase, or word to the group-offered prayer, while others will remain silent, as in any normal group conversation. Silent participation is also meaningful.

TOOLS:

1. Question pages for "assimilation and discussion" are provided for each of the 24 chapters. (These are also printed at the end of "The Messiah Mystery" chapters.)

2. A blank template, to copy in multiples to use as "scratch pages" if desired, for preparing to discuss the questions.

* Permission is given to copy the Discussion questions and the template for educational use.

SECTION I: INTRODUCING THE MESSIAH
Chapter 1   The Genesis of the Messianic Hope

ASSIMILATION* AND DISCUSSION QUESTIONS:

1. What do you think would motivate the Son of God to take the humbling step of taking on human flesh, limiting Himself to a man's body?

2. How creative do you think God has been in his methods of teaching His people? Which of those methods have been most effective in enlisting *your* response?

3. If someone asked you *why* God did not simply force people to accept Him by an act of His will upon ours, what reasons could you give?

4. What residues of the Greek or Hebrew views of history do you see evidence of in modern Western culture or your particular culture? What is your own view of the meaning or goal of history? (If it seems unreasonable to be asked to conceptualize this, try answering it after getting further into this study.)

5. How do you relate to the "root and branch" relationships? As you think of Israel and the Church, which do you think of as the root, which the branch? What sort of interactions have you experienced between them?

6. What aspect of the role of the Messiah means the most to you, or what about Him is interesting you in a new way?

FOR PERSONAL MEDITATION

As individuals, we have great needs for understanding who we are, what life is, and what hope is possible. As you mull over the human predicament, when does being "finite" (limited) most upset you?

With what question about life do you most struggle?

When do you feel most estranged from people or from God?

* To "assimilate" is "to take in and appropriate as nourishment" or "to take into the mind and thoroughly comprehend." These questions are meant to help the reader assimilate the meaning of the chapter. Discussion with others can clarify our own learning and enrich us with new insights from others' viewpoints or experiences.

SECTION I: INTRODUCING THE MESSIAH
Chapter 2:   The Messiah's Arrival

ASSIMILATION AND DISCUSSION QUESTIONS:

1. Imagine *eternity* by conceiving of God's being able to look down upon something in *time, which* is to Him in the eternal present tense, while the human is seeing it as linear, step-by-step.   How does this help you understand the scope of the message of the Bible?

2. If you had been a devout Jew, how do you think you would have reacted to Jesus calling himself "greater than Solomon, Jonah, and Abraham?" (Found in Luke 11:29-32, John 8:51-59) Does this make the charge of blasphemy reasonable?

3. What insights into Jesus' identity does the appearance of Moses and Elijah with Jesus on the mountain (Luke 9:29-36) give you? What hints does it give you about your own immortality?

4. One of the deepest words in scripture is "glory" or "glorify." What is meant? It seems to be of supreme importance to the Father, to the Son, and to the Spirit. What clues do you get from the following passages? (Keep the meaning of "glory" as another marker, as you watch it unfold.)   John 8:48-58, John 13:31,32, John 17:1-5, Luke 24:25-27, John 16:12-15.

5. If we use the pronoun "it" for the Holy Spirit, presumably we are emphasizing His *power.* When we use "He" we are acknowledging His *person.* What is demonstrated in scripture to convince you that the Spirit is indeed a person with separate essence but equal glory with the Father and the Son?

6. The word "trinity" does not appear in the Bible. Why do you think it began to be used? What biblical examples of the convergences of divine presence, overlapping of names, and sharing of glory have most helped you in your own understanding of the "oneness" of God's person? What examples of division in titles, roles, and activities have caused you to see God as "three"?

7. What other questions related to the identity of the Father, Son, and/or Spirit would you like to discuss? What other insights would you like to share?

FOR PERSONAL MEDIATION

What particular evidence of the identity of Jesus have you accepted or rejected? Do you feel you have any sort of "proof" to back up your stance on Jesus? (Use this as an *assimilation* question, not a *discussion* question. Let it serve as a marker as you move on into this study. See how your answers to this question "grow.")

Do you consider yourself "anointed" in the biblical sense? On what basis do you say "yes" or "no"?

SECTION II: THE MESSIAH AND ADAM
Chapter 3:   Adam and Humanity: The Problem of the Fall

ASSIMILATION AND DISCUSSION QUESTIONS

1. What do you think the word "us" in Genesis 1:26 signifies?

2. What in human life most discourages you about "human nature"?

3. How do people today experience Satan's form of temptation (using his technique in Eden) whispering, "Has God said ___?" or perhaps, "You shall not___!" ?

4. What kind of "fig leaves" do we try to appropriate in order to protect ourselves from discovery?

5. Imagine yourself to be Adam or Eve. How might you react to your first experience of seeing death inflicted – by the slaughter of an animal – and then to wrap yourself in its skin?

6. Why might God's promise in Genesis 3:15 be worded "her seed" instead of "his" (the usual carrier of seed)? How did that promise show itself to be important at the time of Jesus' birth?

7. How would you like to live forever in the world as it is right now? Can you find any reason to thank God that Adam and Eve were banned from being allowed to eat from the tree of life in Eden?

FOR PERSONAL MEDITATION

Do you assume you can accomplish being righteous? How do you respond to C.H. Mackintosh's view on our inability to do so?

How do you experience being "in Adam" or "in Christ"? Adam was rejected from Eden. What does it mean to you to be "accepted in the Beloved"?

If you met Adam in heaven, what might you like to say to him? Ask him?

SECTION II: THE MESSIAH AND ADAM
Chapter 4:   The Second Adam as Son and Bridegroom

ASSIMILATION AND DISCUSSION QUESTIONS

1. Has your understanding of the gospel of Jesus Christ been more heavily weighted on Christ's work to nullify the "negative" problem of man's sin or on His work to open up the "positive" purpose of man's redemption? About which do you feel most need for revelation right now?

2. Looking back to "before the beginning," we can draw some conclusions from the biblical understanding of the eternal Godhead's inner relationship. Does insight into the relationships of the Trinity give you any better grasp of humanity's being "in God's image"? If we compare ourselves with animals, what is different? What are we uniquely capable of, drawn to?

3. How have you usually defined "the church"? If you are seeing anything different about the church through this study of Adam and Christ, what would it be?

4. Israel is made analogous to God's "wife" in the Old Testament. (Examples: In the book of Ruth with its theme of a "kinsman redeemer"; in Ezekiel, such as in chapter 16; and in Hosea's references to "faithfulness" or "unfaithfulness.") Why do you think the church on earth is called Christ's "bride" rather than "wife"? (She is called the "Lamb's wife" after the Marriage Feast.) Why might God have chosen the analogy of "bride" to depict the intimate relationship of the church with the *incarnational* (physical) manifestation of God the Son? How might progression or timing have been factors in God's choice of metaphorical names for "the believers" at different periods of history?

5. Just how close to God do "the redeemed" ultimately come? How does that position compare with Adam and Eve's closeness? Do you think God may have "worked all things together for good" (Romans 8:28) even in the Fall?

FOR PERSONAL MEDITATION:

Our "sonship" (and daughtership) destiny (Eph. 1:5,6) is bestowed on us "*in* the Beloved Son." If you think you have entered into "the Beloved," how or when were you made aware of this being accomplished?

Do you expect to be present at the Marriage Feast of the Lamb? What emotions does that prospect cause in you?

Is your spontaneous response to the promise of the Messiah's soon return, "Come!"? If not, why do you suppose that is?

SECTION III: THE MESSIAH AND ABRAHAM
Chapter 5:   The Mystery of the Covenant

ASSIMILATION AND DISCUSSION QUESTIONS

1. What would account for the unity of the various covenants?

2. How did God mercifully provide for man's weakness in keeping covenants made with Him?

3. On what basis is Abraham considered the forefather of Judaism, Islam, and Christianity?

4. In what ways did Jesus qualify to contend for the title of "the promised seed of Abraham," the Messiah?

5. What was Jesus' relationship to Abraham as stated in John 8:56-58? What do you think Jesus' short sentence (John 8:58) about Abraham and about Himself really means?

6. What does *the resurrection* have to do with Christ being accepted as the promised one through whom the world would be blessed?

7. What unanswered questions do you continue to have about Abraham, the covenant, or "the seed"?

FOR PERSONAL MEDITATION:

When or how did you realize your "heirship" – becoming one of Abraham's offspring, "an heir according to the promise"? (This is shown to be possible even for a Gentile, in Galatians 3:23-29.)

Do you look forward to "sitting down with Abraham, Isaac, and Jacob" among the accepted "children of the promise?" (Consider carefully Jesus' warning to Israelites after His interview with the Gentile centurion at Capernaum. See Matthew 8:5-13.) On what basis do you expect, or not expect, to sit down with them?

SECTION III: THE MESSIAH AND ABRAHAM
Chapter 6:   The Mystery on Mt. Moriah

ASSIMILATION AND DISCUSSION QUESTIONS

1. What emotions do you think might have flooded over you on Mt. Moriah, had you been Abraham? Isaac? God the Father? Christ the Son?

2. Why do you think Abraham was able to take action on Mt. Moriah in obedience to the command?

3. Why do you think God required this of Abraham?

4. What hint does the Holy Spirit give us in Hebrews 11:19 about what Abraham believed about God, which might have enabled him to risk slaying his son?

5. What relationship do you see between the two occasions on Mt. Moriah, and the Messianic prophecy in Isaiah 53?

6. What significance do you attribute to the geographical location of Abraham's sacrifice of his son, and God's sacrifice of His?

7. What do you think is the relationship between *faith* and the good *works* accompanying righteous living that are obviously God's desire for his people?

FOR PERSONAL MEDITATION

How do you find Abraham a help to you in discovering what kind of righteousness pleases God?

Have you ever felt you were asked to "slay your Isaac"?

SECTION IV: THE MESSIAH AND MOSES
Chapter 7:   The Relationship between Moses and the Messiah

ASSIMILATION AND DISCUSSION QUESTIONS

1. How might you compare and contrast the roles of Abraham and Moses?

2. Based on the text, what would you see as the theme of the book of Exodus?

3. What foundations were laid in the Exodus period (which includes Leviticus, Numbers, Deuteronomy), and continue to reappear in the following centuries?

4. Of what is the Passover a picture? What does it commemorate? How might today's Jews and Christians emphasize two different aspects of the Passover?

5. How were Moses' and Christ's mediating roles similar? Different?

6. What pre-planted redemptive analogy made John the Baptist's announcement of the Messiah immediately perceivable to the Jews?

7. How does Don Richardson's experience with the Sawi people highlight what is necessary for communicating the gospel of Jesus Christ?

8. What various elements of Christ's passion week were foreshadowed by the Passover in Egypt? In time, which came first, Moses' Passover or Christ's? In God's eternal plan, which came first?

9. How is Christ shown to supersede Moses? (Especially consider insights from the first three chapters of book of Hebrews.)

10. With what attitude did Jesus speak of Moses?

11. What did Jesus' raising the standard *higher than the law* point out about humanity? (i.e. "Moses said . . . but I say . . .") What did it point out about Himself?

12. What can we learn about Jesus and about Moses from their conference on the Mt. of Transfiguration?

FOR PERSONAL MEDITATION

Is Jesus your mediator?

Luke 24:25-27 might be the key verse of this book. How "slow of heart" have you been? How willing are you to accept the testimony of Moses and the prophets according to the Messiah's interpretation?

SECTION IV: THE MESSIAH AND MOSES
Chapter 8:   The Covenants of Law and Grace

ASSIMILATION AND DISCUSSION QUESTIONS

1. What kind of covenant was the one God made with Abraham?

2. What kind of covenant was the one God established with Israel on Mt. Sinai?

3. Who instituted the "new covenant"? Who had mentioned it centuries before?

4. What did the law do for the Hebrew community, or for the world?

5. How do Mt. Sinai and Mt. Calvary typify the covenants of law and grace?

6. What does the New Testament say the spiritual purpose of the law is?

7. How does the covenant of grace refer back to the covenant of promise instead of the covenant of law, according to Romans 4? Why?

8. What is the fresh principle of the new covenant, which is introduced by the Holy Spirit?

9. What significance is found in the timing of the cross, resurrection, and enthronement of Christ in relationship to the yearly Jewish feasts?

10. How did the new relationship (made available by the completed work of the Messiah) become visible the day of the cross – right in the Temple?

11. What sorts of reasons does the book of Hebrews give for the superior excellence of the new covenant over the old?

12. Why do you suppose the Israelites and we, too, find it hard to live by faith, and often prefer clear-cut laws?

FOR PERSONAL MEDITATION

Do you find yourself avoiding God's law, or giving up because you're not able to keep it, or taking pride in relative success in keeping it? Do you find any of these responses to be spiritually healthy?

What keys are you finding to the biblical place of law and grace for your own life?

SECTION V: THE MESSIAH AND THE TABERNACLE
Chapter 9:   The Tabernacle: God's Provided Way of Acceptance

ASSIMILATION AND DISCUSSION QUESTIONS

1. What function does the Tabernacle serve in God's relationship with His people?

2. Look over the description of the Tabernacle in Exodus 25-31. Note the materials God asks the people to contribute (25:1-9), and the careful descriptions of measurements, materials, workmanship, ordination, garments, sabbaths, and feasts that God gives them in exact pattern. Hebrews 9:23,24 gives spiritual insight on these "patterns" (KJV) or "copies" (RSV). *What* did they actually "pattern," or "copy"?

3. What is the basic physical purpose of each of the seven pieces of furniture used in the Tabernacle?

4. One may use the progression through the Tabernacle to present the *good news of God's acceptance* to a seeker by sharing the meaning of the symbols – (progressing from the door of the Tabernacle court to the altar and laver; to the Holy Place with its light and bread and altar of intercession; and finally to the Most Holy Place, wherein is the Ark and the Mercy Seat). How does each one of the seven symbols teach the order and meaning of acceptance with God?

5. Think of examples of "telescopic" (broad) and "microscopic" (detailed) study which have helped you in the past. What *subject* related to the Tabernacle might you wish to explore microscopically in the future?

6. What insight has most enriched your life as you've studied the Old Testament Tabernacle?

FOR PERSONAL MEDITATION

As you present yourself before God, how have you, or do you *personally participate* in the meanings represented by each of these seven symbols?

SECTION V: THE TABERNACLE AND THE MESSIAH
Chapter 10:   The Messiah Fulfills the Tabernacle's Purpose

ASSIMILATION AND DISCUSSION QUESTIONS

1. How has Jesus fulfilled the message and work of the Tabernacle? (Hebrews 7:23-10:25 helps interpret this.)

2. Looking at Hebrews, on what basis would you say that the Messiah is . . .
    a better sacrifice?
    a better sanctification?
    a better priest?
    a better priesthood?
    a better result?

3. How does Revelation parallel with the Tabernacle? (Especially see: candlesticks, Revelation 1:12; worthy is the Lamb, Rev. 4:5-14; tent of witness, Rev. 15:5; no lamp, Rev. 22:5; no temple, Rev. 21:22.)

4. What are the believer's spiritual sacrifices today? (See Romans 12:1, Exodus 33:7-10, and Hebrews 13:10-15.)

5. From Hebrews 9, what does Jesus' resurrection and ascension into heaven have to do with the Tabernacle, especially the Day of Atonement?

6. How might we see the Tabernacle as a picture of <u>finding initial acceptance with God,</u> (moving from the outer court on through to the Mercy Seat)?

7. How might we also see the Tabernacle as an outline or progression for <u>the believer's on-going worship</u>?

8. How might we see the Tabernacle as a pictorial overview of <u>the Christian life</u>?

9. What New Testament insight about the Messiah's fulfillment of the Tabernacle's meanings do you think will be most helpful to your own spiritual life?

FOR PERSONAL MEDITATION

In what relationship to the Messiah do you stand, as you consider the witness of the Father to the Son, as expressed in I John 5:9-13?

If you have accepted God's invitation to approach Him through the sacrifice of the Lamb of God, to what extent do you continue on with the Tabernacle's deeper meanings for "the priesthood of believers" in the area of *worship*?

SECTION VI: THE MESSIAH AND THE FEASTS
Chapter 11:   Time, Sevens, the Sabbath, and the Lord of the Sabbath

ASSIMILATION AND DISCUSSION QUESTIONS

1. What are some of the patterns discernible in God's use of time?

2. Why does Judaism call itself "a religion of time"?

3. Where did "the sabbath" come from?

4. What seem to be some of God's purposes in creating the sabbath?

5. What did Christ's conflict with religious authorities over "sabbath keeping" reveal about His attitudes and His identity?

6. What striking chastisement demonstrated God's holding Israel responsible for keeping the sabbaths of the land?

7. What experiences have you had with the sabbath as a principle, or a day, or an experience shared with Jewish or Christian groups that observe the seventh day sabbath?

8. If the seventh day symbolizes a finished creation and the first a finished redemption, what day would most fittingly symbolize the future Marriage Feast of the Lamb?

9. Hebrews 4:9 says "So then, there remains a sabbath rest for the people of God." What do you think is meant?

FOR PERSONAL MEDITATION

Have you, do you, or do you yet expect to experience the "rest" of Hebrews 4:9?

What aspects of your own life do you sense are related to the practice and problem of religious legalism?

What personal needs do you sense that seem to be related to the principles of the sabbath, or of spiritual rest?

SECTION VI: THE MESSIAH AND THE FEASTS
Chapter 12:   The Feasts of God's Year and of Eternity

ASSIMILATION AND DISCUSSION QUESTIONS

1. What seems to be the meaning of sevens in the Bible?

2. What may the "eighth day" signify?

3. What factors have heightened interest in eschatology in recent decades?

4. What do the feasts have to do with culture (especially agriculture), with religious practice, with eschatology?

5. What clues to the Messiah are found in the feast of Passover and Unleavened Bread?

6. What in the third feast is parallel to the Resurrection of Christ from the dead?

7. What seems to be the "typical" meaning of the fourth, the summer harvest feast?

8. Which feasts appear to be fulfilled, and which unfulfilled? Where does that seem to position us on God's calendar?

9. What is your experience of applying the principles or practice of the feasts to your own life? Which, or what, has become most meaningful to you?

FOR PERSONAL MEDITATION

What role are you playing in the spiritual completion of *Shavuot,* the Summer Feast of Ingathering?

With what emotions, hopes, or dreads, do you anticipate the spiritual completion of the Fall Feasts – the Second Coming of the Messiah?

SECTION VII: THE MESSIAH AND DAVID
Chapter 13:   Christ the Son of David

ASSIMILATION AND DISCUSSION QUESTIONS

1. What is the background behind David's respect for "the Lord's anointed"?

2. G. Campbell Morgan sees two major themes in the Bible. What are they? He recognizes three movements, or human longings, in the Old Testament taken separately. What are they?

3. How did God's early history with Israel express itself in a spiritual *theocracy* rather than the monarchical forms of Gentile nations?

4. How did David's attitude toward leadership cooperate or coincide with God's underlying Kingship?

5. What parallels do you find between David and Christ? Consider their genealogical line, their attitudes, and the details of their histories.

6. What evidence might be found that Jesus was steeped in the Psalms of His forefather, David?

7. What promises did God make to David? Which have been fulfilled, and which remain unfulfilled?

8. What clues to Jesus' being a *king* do you find in His bloodline, in the circumstances surrounding His conception and birth, in His teachings, in the clues found in the events (and words) of Passion Week and His crucifixion.

9. How is the Kingdom of God different from earthly kingdoms?

FOR PERSONAL MEDITATION

Have I purposely made the King of kings my own sovereign and Lord?

If I have, how does that substantially change my life?

SECTION VII: THE MESSIAH AND DAVID
Chapter 14:   Christ and the Kingship

ASSIMILATION AND DISCUSSION QUESTIONS

1. What characterized the revolutionary kind of kingdom Jesus taught about?

2. Why do you think Jesus taught in parables?

3. What evidence does scripture give that Jesus' disciples as well as the people saw Him as the "Son of David" and expected Him to capitalize on the Messianic title and rule?

4. What evidences did Jesus give that He expected His own rejection and execution?

5. What kind of warnings did Jesus give about the Kingdom of God?

6. What evidences manifesting Christ's kingship during the week of His Passion might we recognize?

7. What do you think was the crux of Christ's struggle in Gethsemane?

8. What evidences do we have from the Acts and Letters that the early believers thought of Jesus as their King?

9. How did they interpret Psalm 2 and Psalm 110, and use them to identify Jesus?

10. What various glimpses does Revelation give of the glorified Son of God as King?

11. What is the tone of the culminating feast in Revelation? Of His many roles, which is the Messiah manifesting at that marvelous feast?

FOR PERSONAL MEDITATION

How thoroughly do I embrace Jesus' kingdom principles in my life?

What do I expect my identification with this King to cost me . . . or reward me?

SECTION VIII: THE MESSIAH AND THE PROPHETS
Chapter 15:   Prophets and Prophecy in the Old Testament

ASSIMILATION AND DISCUSSION QUESTIONS

1. What do you see as the tie between Elijah and John the Baptist?

2. What evidence do you see for mankind's "quest for a prophet," to use G. Campbell Morgan's phrase?

3. How was the Hebrew attitude about kingship different from other nations?

4. What was the relationship between kings and prophets in Israel?

5. What was the relationship between Israel's prophets and priests?

6. What kind of messages did true prophets deliver? How would you characterize some of their different modes and moods?

7. To what various time periods may prophecy refer?

8. How would you like to have been called to be a prophet? What kinds of things were difficult for them?

FOR PERSONAL MEDITATION

What particular warnings from the prophets do I take to heart?

What promises of God through the prophets am I counting upon as a personal hope?

Do I ever have a sense of sharing in the pathos of God?

SECTION VIII: THE MESSIAH AND THE PROPHETS
Chapter 16: Christ the Prophecy and the Prophet

ASSIMILATION AND DISCUSSION QUESTIONS

1. What impresses you about the tie between the last prophet's prophecies and the introduction to the New Testament? (See Malachi 4:6 related to Luke l: 16,17; and Malachi 3:l related to Luke 7:26,27.)

2. What details of the life and death of Jesus do you find in Isaiah 52:13-53:12? Do you find it reasonable to apply it to Him? Did He? Did the Apostles?

3. Psalm 110:l is repeatedly quoted in the New Testament. How do you understand its importance to Jesus and to the early believers?

4. At Pentecost, Peter said Joel 2:28-33 was being seen. Who do you think gave Peter the authority to say that?

5. Melchizedek appears only in Genesis 14 and eight times in Hebrews. How does the Spirit of God use Melchizedek as the precedent to authenticate Jesus' priesthood? Who do you think gave the writer of Hebrews that insight?

6. Remembering Dauermann's example of prophecy as a bull's-eye which narrows down a field to establish identity, do you think the chances of the seven circles of certainty being hit by anyone but Jesus of Nazareth are very likely?

7. How does the scripture tie Moses and Jesus together as prophets?

8. How did Jesus share in the role of the prophets?

9. How was Jesus different from other prophets?

10. What span and realm of prophecy did Jesus put forth – beyond the vision of Old Testament prophets?

FOR PERSONAL MEDITATION

What warnings from Jesus the prophet do I take seriously?

What hopes engendered by Christ's prophetic promises am I counting on?

SECTION IX: THE MESSIAH MANIFESTED
Chapter 17:   The Life of Jesus the Christ

ASSIMILATION AND DISCUSSION QUESTIONS

1. How do the four presentations of the life of Jesus help give us more fullness than a single account? How do the four Gospels differ?

2. From the samples found in Matthew eight and nine, what are some of your impressions of Jesus' daily life? (Consider the sheer volume of interactions; the display of His power, character, and divinity; the facts, attitudes, and burdens Jesus expressed, etc.)

3. Had you been on the scene seeing this man in action, *who* do you think you would have thought the man to be?

4. What characteristics stand out to you in Jesus' personality or character?

5. How did people respond to Him? (Consider the response of the sick, the poor, women, children, the religious leadership, the men Jesus traveled with, etc.)

6. What evidences do you see for Christ having a sense of humor?

7. How effectively do you see Jesus the teacher using discourse, dialogue, parables, etc.? What examples stand out in your mind?

8. What do Jesus' miracles signify – about the identity of the one performing them, about the nature of God's power, about His love?

FOR PERSONAL MEDITATION

If Jesus faced you with the question, "Who do you say I am?" what would you answer Him?

Having seen where Jesus' life led, and having heard His warning that following Him would be costly, how would you be willing to answer that question about His identity before the watching world?

SECTION IX: THE MESSIAH MANIFESTED
Chapter 18:   The Death and Resurrection of Jesus the Christ

ASSIMILATION AND DISCUSSION QUESTIONS

1. Why did Jesus so "desire to eat *this* Passover" (the one before the cross) with His disciples?

2. What might you have expected of Jesus, had you been one of the twelve disciples? How might you have reacted to His passivity as He entered Jerusalem, or His non-resistance the night of His arrest?

3. What do you think the title "King of the Jews" meant to Jesus, to the disciples, to Pilate, to the crowd? What does it mean to you?

4. How would you tell someone the meaning of Jesus' "passion"? How does Henri Nouwen's meditation on the Lord's passion help you fathom it?

5. What do you think was happening on the cross? Beyond the physical torture, what was Jesus going through?

6. What do you think might be the meaning of Jesus' cry on the cross, echoing Psalm 22?

7. *How* does the cross deliver a person from the human predicament?

8. Had you been Thomas, what might you have felt that night when the risen Lord invited you to touch His wounds?

9. Scripture records what characteristics of the Christ's resurrected body?

10. On what basis is a miracle credible, according to Dorothy Sayers or C. S. Lewis?

11. What difference does the resurrection of Christ really make as a person faces death?

FOR PERSONAL MEDITATON

Are you convinced that Jesus truly died, was buried, and was raised from death? If in truth he did not, was not, then what do you think of him – his reliability, his sanity? If the resurrection is a lie, who was Jesus?

Subjectively, have you appropriated the benefits of Christ's sacrifice to your own life? That is, (according to Watchman Nee's explanation) are you willing to see the *blood* as <u>God</u> sees it, as satisfactory propitiation for the sins of the world? And are you willing to accept the *cross* as <u>you</u> see it, as your own death penalty paid by Christ?

SECTION X: THE MESSIAH'S GIFT: THE HOLY SPIRIT
Chapter 19: Christ's Enthronement and the Gift of the Holy Spirit

ASSIMILATION AND DISCUSSION QUESTIONS

1. After the shock of the resurrection, what was signified by the next astounding event on God's calendar, Pentecost?

2. Considering what was presented in Chapter VI on the Feasts of Israel, how do you think Pentecost initiated fulfillment of the meanings symbolized in *Shavuot,* the fourth feast?

3. Considering the miraculous manifestations, the message delivered at Pentecost, and the people represented there – who was the source of this outpouring, what was the promise being fulfilled, and to whom?

4. On the night before His death, what preparation did Jesus give the disciples for the arrival of the Holy Spirit among them in a new way? Who would He be to them? Why, or in what way, could He be "better" than Jesus?

5. How was the power of the Holy Spirit manifested, and what were some of the results during the first few weeks after Pentecost?

6. What lay behind the disciples' use of "the name of Jesus"? How significant is the name of Jesus to our own acceptance before the Father?

7. How has the name "Christ" somewhat diminished the meaning of the Messiah's title? What more does "Messiah" communicate?

8. What does the Holy Spirit have to do with the scriptures? Consider the scriptures' source, their interpretation, and their power.

FOR PERSONAL MEDITATION

Do I appreciate the Spirit of God's role in giving me the scriptures?

Do I purposely depend upon the Spirit to reveal Christ to me, invite Him to do so, thank Him for revelation?

Do I ever come to the point of awe before the Holy Spirit, realizing He is equally deserving worship, along with the Son and the Father?

SECTION X: THE MESSIAH'S GIFT: THE HOLY SPIRIT
Chapter 20:   The Teaching and Indwelling Spirit

ASSIMILATION AND DISCUSSION QUESTIONS

1. What re-ignited the faith and courage of the disciples after the crucifixion?

2. How would you summarize "the kernel" of the Gospel the disciples spread? What scriptures would help you summarize their message to someone?

3. What is the particular teaching role of the Letters? That is, what do the Epistles offer us in contrast to the function of the four Gospels or Acts?

4. Why do the historical record of Acts and the spiritual teachings of the Letters not seem to lead the Church to total uniformity in doctrine or liturgy?

5. How do infant baptism and immersion baptism reflect different aspects of biblical truth?

6. How are the Old and New Covenant "seals" similar, but different?

7. What do you think the "until" indicates in Ephesians 1:14 and I Corinthians 11:26?

8. Why do you think the word "Trinity" was coined? Do you think it was justified?

FOR PERSONAL MEDITATION

Have you experienced in your own life an intimate connection between the written word of God and its author, the Holy Spirit?

What spiritual fruits and gifts do you personally sense to be growing out of your relationship to the indwelling Spirit, or poured out upon you by Him?

SECTION XI: THE MESSIAH'S COMMUNITY
Chapter 21:   Relationships within the Messianic Community:
**   Root and Branches (Israel and Gentile Christians)**

ASSIMILATION AND DISCUSSION QUESTIONS

1. What role did persecution seem to play in bursting the geographic and racial boundaries of the messianic community?

2. What examples of reaching people "in Jerusalem, Judea, Samaria, and to the ends of the earth" do we find in the book of Acts?

3. What unusual methods did God use to direct Peter, and to call and later give a special apostleship to Paul?

4. What roles do Peter and Paul especially play in the spreading of the gospel of Jesus the Christ?

5. What precedent did the Jerusalem Council set, which would have far-reaching effects?

6. What role did the Letters to the young churches play in the life of the messianic community? Who wrote them, and to whom?

7. What did "jealousy" have to do with all this? Who is "the remnant"? What are we to remember about the "root" and "branch"?

8. What did Pentecost have to do with demonstrating God's plan?

9. Of whom is the "one new man" made up?

10. What happened to separate messianic Jewish believers away from both Jewish and later the Christian communities?

11. What do you expect Israel's role to be in the future?

FOR PERSONAL MEDITATION

How do you feel about being part of the remnant – either part of the "root" or of the "branch"?

What do you personally think about the attempt to heal the rift between Jews and Christians and Messianic Jews today? What part would you like to have in that?

SECTION XI: THE MESSIAH'S COMMUNITY
Chapter 22:   Relationships between the Messiah and His People

ASSIMILATION AND DISCUSSIONS QUESTIONS

1. What life story or particular experience has especially communicated to you the *cost* of discipleship?

2. How do you understand the meaning of the believer's union with Christ? How important to *God* is the believer's "inclusion"? How important to the *believer* is being "in Christ"?

3. Why do you think God might have given us so many analogies for His Son's relationship with His people?

4. What does the Church's being "the body of Christ" mean to you?

5. What examples of Old Testament terminology do you notice in New Testament pictures of the believers as "a living temple"?

6. Why is the New Testament form of "the temple" fitted for the circumstances of history since 70 AD?

7. Biblically, what is the spiritual inheritance of "co-heirs with Christ"?

8. How do Israel and the Church approach their message to the world differently? What two key words pinpoint the difference?

9. Do you find helpful Newbigin's understanding of the Church as the *locus* rather than the agent of mission? Why?

10. If Christians are to be soldiers of the King, who is the enemy? Why is it important to rightly identify the enemy?

11. How do you respond to finding the love relationship to be the relational analogy with which we are left at the end of the Bible?

FOR PERSONAL MEDITATION

Which of the six analogies picturing Christ's relationship with His own is most meaningful to you? With which do you feel you have the least experience? Do you think they are true even if not "felt"? Which do you feel the greatest need to "reckon" true?

SECTION XII: THE MESSIANIC CONSUMMATION
Chapter 23: The Church, the World, and Closing Traumas

ASSIMILATION AND DISCUSSION QUESTIONS

1. Why do you think the elements of the Lord's Supper are the center of worship on earth? What does Revelation show to be the center in heaven?

2. How does Jesus appear in the introduction to Revelation? What surrounds Him? What does His garb suggest about the role He is manifesting as He gives the messages of this book?

3. What new role do we see Jesus manifesting in the latter chapters of Revelation? Why have we not seen Him fully in that role before?

4. What scripture do you think is a good example of the triple application of a prophetic message (i.e. one speaking to a local situation, having a wider application, and yet a future fulfillment)?

5. How would you summarize the major admonitions of Revelation's letters to the seven churches?

6. How are heaven and earth contrasted in the central section of Revelation? What is happening in each location?

7. How is the number *seven* used in Revelation? What do you think it signifies?

8. Why does no drawn-out battle between Good and Evil appear at the climax of the end-time traumas? When was the battle really fought? How do you find Eller's quotation on "things are not as they appear" helpful in understanding the present power of the Enemy?

9. Why do you think God is justified in saying He is not *ashamed* to be called the God of those who have suffered? (Hebrews 11:16) What is ahead for them?

FOR PERSONAL MEDITATION

How have you responded to Christ's plea in Revelation 3:20?

Do you really think life's struggles are "worth it all" for a believer?

How do you feel personally about worshipping the Lamb – now and in heaven?

SEDTION XII: THE MESSIANIC CONSUMMATION
Chapter 24   The King, the Bride, and the Kingdom

ASSIMILATION AND DISCUSSION QUESTIONS

1. What special meanings might the risen Lord's promise to return *"soon"* hold?

2. What does the clue in Matthew 24:14 indicate about the timing of Lord's return?

3. What kind of warnings did Jesus give about the culmination of history when He was on earth?

4. What clues do you find in scripture about the identity of the Bride of Christ? *Who* will make up the Messiah's Bride?

5. What do the closing words of each of the Lord's letters to the seven churches (in Revelation 2 and 3) prompt in the reader?

6. Compared with the condition of Adam's bride, Eve, what is to be the destiny of the Second Adam's wife, the Church?

7. How does the Bride display what has always been God's eternal purpose?

FOR PERSONAL MEDITATION

Beside Jesus, whom do you think you will especially want to meet in heaven?

Does your spirit sing, "Come! Come, Lord Jesus!" ?

TEMPLATE: RESPONSES TO ASSIMILATION
AND DISCUSSION QUESTIONS

T

Section:
Chapter:

Name:
Date:

Notations:

1.

2.

3.

4.

5.

6.

7.

8.

9.

10

11.

12.

Additional notations, questions, additions, etc.:

ALTERNATIVE C:

GROUP STUDY BASED ON FOCUS PAGES:

This mode of study fits groups who either do not have the textbook or have only a short time to study, such as a 40-minute Bible class. The teacher needs to be well versed in the Bible and "The Messiah Mystery" text, so as to be able to set the stage clearly, and amplify meanings when needed. Group feedback and discussion are key aspects to real engagement with the content and its practical implications. The leader will need to creatively tailor the broad possibilities into a pattern that is do-able in the time frame allowed.

USES FOR THE FOCUS PAGES

1. These pages using seven approaches to a topic provide the leader with content and a pattern for study sessions. Less overwhelming than the textbook, a one-page handout can help the student focus on one of the 24 topics in "The Messiah Mystery" and base their research on scripture. (KEY picture, FOCUS statement, and SEARCH scripture passages help to focus the study.)

2. The pages provide thoughtful questions for considering what God is communicating and how it impacts our faith and our lives. *What does the scripture mean, and what does it mean to me?* (THINK and DIGEST questions provide a basis for class discussion.)

3. The focus needs to move to an active response to the Spirit of God. *How am I to respond, what is being asked of me?* (The APPLY questions are quite personal, and call for honesty. Unless volunteered spontaneously, these answers need not be shared in class sessions.)

4. The author's worship response is found in the PRAYER. It may become an invitation to the reader to be open before God. *How might the Spirit guide me to speak to God about this matter? What does this mean to Him?*

Procedure: It is helpful to start in the introductory class with an overview of the topics and an introduction to the "Shadow and Substance" method. The leader introduces the next week's topic at the end of one session, and directs the class to prepare for discussion the next week, using the Focus Page and a template. Participants study the scriptures listed in the SEARCH section, think through the THINK and DIGEST sections, and hopefully pray through the APPLY questions and the PRAYER. The next week, the leader helps the group focus on the topic, teaches and amplifies as felt necessary, and leads a discussion.

Timing: Using the Focus Page format with a group that meets weekly, it will probably require a minimum of 7 months, or 8 months with breaks. September to May works well with the rhythms of the U.S. calendar year.

Providing the pages: The Focus Pages enhance personal research and give continuity for the participant who has to miss a class. Focus Pages can either be handed out weekly, or the leader may copy all the pages and bind them as a unified lesson plan, preceded by a "Chapter and Date" schedule. The packet would become a 28-page collection: the schedule, the two "Shadow and Substance" explanation pages, the 24 Focus Pages, and a template response page. One other possibility is for class members to purchase "Keys to the Messiah Mystery."

TOOLS:
1. A two-sided handout briefly summarizing the "Shadow and Substance" concept is printed on pages 73-74. A fuller explanation of the "Shadow and Substance" concept can be found on pages 18-23 in Part II of the KEYS, or in Chapter 5 of "The Messiah Mystery."
2. Focus Pages for discussion of the 24 topics of "The Messiah Mystery" are found on pages 75-98 of the KEYS.
3. One blank template to write down Focus Page responses is found on page 99.

Permission is given to copy the "Shadow and Substance" handouts, Focus Pages, and Template for educational use.

THE "SHADOW AND SUBSTANCE" CONCEPT IN BRIEF

LOCATION The "shadow and substance" concept is introduced in Chapter 5 of "The Messiah Mystery." It is pictured in the "Shadow and Substance" diagram on page 49 of the text and page 74 of the leaders' resource, "Keys to the Messiah Mystery." Part II of the "Keys" explains the method in detail.

EXPLANATION The Messiah Mystery's panoramic look at the scriptures employs a way of looking at the broad sweep of history as a "shadow and substance" progression. The term comes out of Colossians 2:17 RSV: "These are only a shadow of what is to come; but the substance belongs to Christ." Other translations use "reality" for "substance." The Spirit of God uses this terminology in Romans 5:14, Hebrews 8:7 and 10:1, etc.

EXAMPLES The "reality" spoken of refers either to the incarnated Lord Jesus' completion of a shadowy type, or the actual reality in God's presence. A reality – like a tree – casts a shadow in which a person can walk forward toward the reality. Examples: Adam was called a "type" of the Second Adam, Christ. Abraham's sacrifice of Isaac was a shadow or "type" of the Father's sacrifice of the Son, both on Mt. Moriah. The Law is called "the shadow of what was to come." The Tabernacle was constructed "exactly" according to God's pattern of the reality in heaven.

FAITH BUILDING When we are alert to the scripture's shadows and realities, we get a feel for God's eternal purposes. We are awed to look at history from His viewpoint, from above, looking at time from eternity. Our confidence in the completion of His purposes grows. We realize that we ourselves are somewhere along the line of this human pilgrimage, and we want to get our bearing for where we are, and how we fit into God's amazing plan.

AMAZING CONCLUSIONS When we grasp the essence of a shadow and its completed reality, we appreciate both in deeper ways. For example, God's desire to dwell ("tabernacle") among His people is a major theme that moves through the whole Bible. One of the major shadows of the Old Covenant is a picture of how access to God was mercifully provided in the whole sacrificial system and the Aaronic priesthood, centered in Tabernacle or Temple worship. Then came the Incarnation! John 1:14 uses tabernacle language when it says the Word of God became flesh and dwelled ("tabernacled") among us. When the perfect Lamb of God gasped, "It is finished," the need for the Temple was finished. At the Son's exaltation, the symbol of God's Presence came forth from heaven (and perhaps from the Mercy Seat in the Temple). Fire appeared on the heads of believers. In the New Covenant, believers became "temples of the Holy Spirit," corporately becoming a holy building, with Christ as the cornerstone.

AWAKENING TO CLUES As we learn to look for shadows and fulfillments, we are awed by the intricacy and beauty and certainty of God's eternal purpose. We worship!

TOOL The Master Circle that demonstrates this way of looking at scripture in "shadow and substance" terms is printed on the back of this page.

Permission is given to copy this page, the S and S diagram, and all the following Focus Pages, for educational purposes.

THE MESSIAH: Preparation & Consummation

SUBSTANCE

New Testament   *Colossians 2:17*

Witness of Cross & Resurrection

Witness of Works

Witness of Enthronement

Suffering
Dying
Rising

Life
Character
Miracles

Enthronement in
Heaven
Holy Spirit poured forth
Coming of the Kingdom

Witness of Words

VALIDATION

VINDICATION

Witness of Believers

Testimony of God
Testimony of Men

RECOGNITION

7   8   9

EXALTATION

Jew and Gentile made
one body in Christ
The Holy Spirit continues to
reveal and empower

6   *Identity and*   10

Meaning of   PROCLAMATION

CHARACTERIZATION   *the Messiah*   5

Pre-figuring in Lives

Adam
Abraham and Isaac
Moses
David
Prophets

1

CELEBRATION

2

PROPITIATION

3

EXPECTATION

4

SYMBOLIZATION

Code Words
Numbers
Names
Titles

Preplanted in Clues

Circumcision

Sabbaths
Jubilee
Feasts

The priesthood
The kingship

Altars
Tabernacle
Ark
Temple

The Law
Covenants
Prophecies

Panoramas in Time

Promises in Words

Portrayals in Space

SHADOW

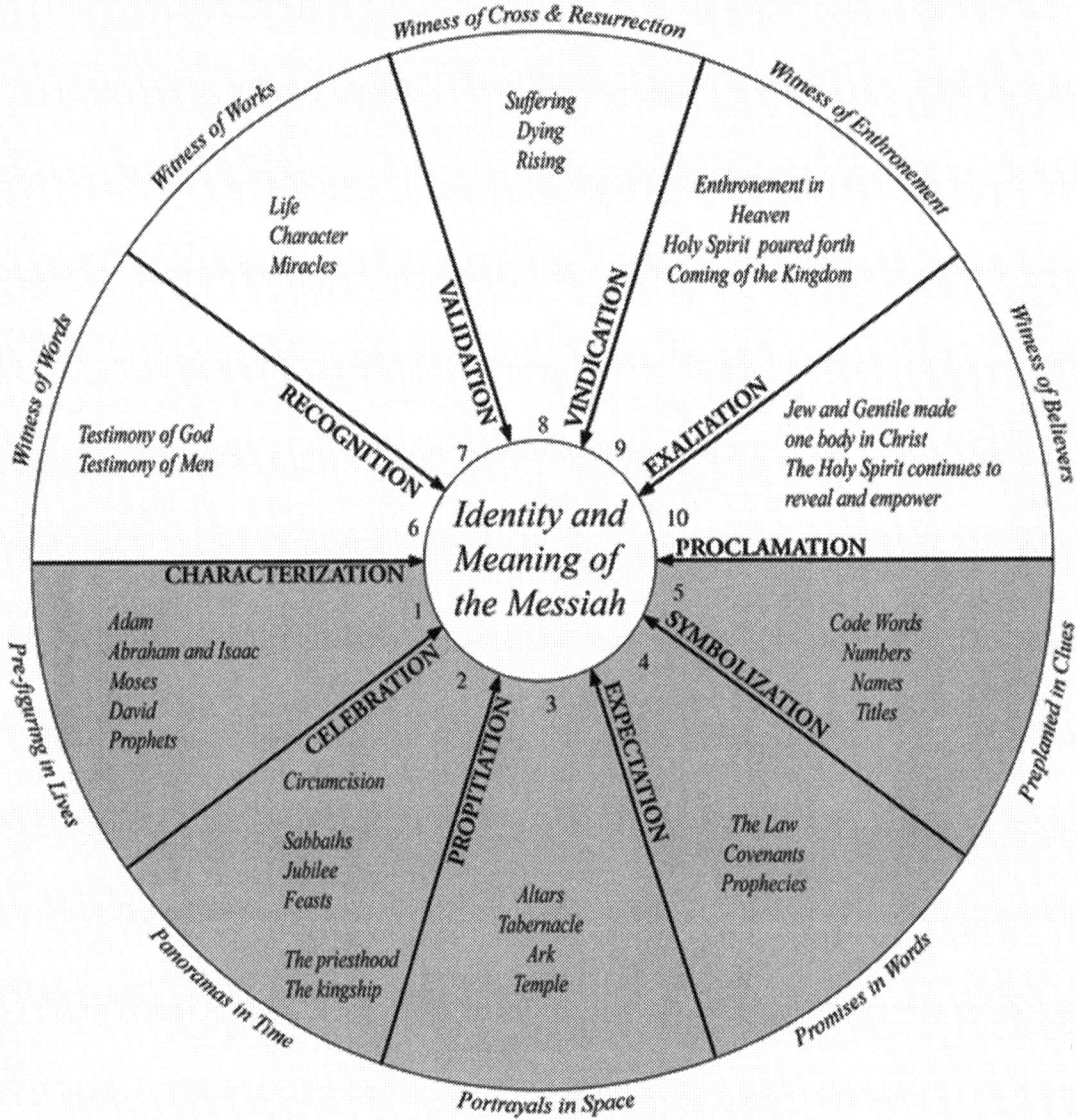

Old Testament   *Hebrews 8:5, 10:1*

Dawn of hope

> Focus: *Our Struggle*. Man is in a hopeless predicament, but God has provided an answer. He means for each of us to discover the identity of His anointed Messiah, the Father's unique offer of hope for humanity.

Search:

• "Anointed" in English is translated "messiah" in Hebrew. Who did God anoint? See Leviticus 4:3, 1 Kings 19:1516, I Samuel 10:1, 16:1-13, II Samuel 23:1, Acts 4:26 (with Psalm 2:2), Acts 10:36-38.

• Why does the world need the ultimate messiah? See Romans 3:23-28, Ephesians 2:1-7.

• What early glimpses of hope were given to Adam and Eve (Genesis 3:15), to Abraham (Genesis 12:3), to David (Psalm 2 and Psalm 110 quoted in Hebrews 5:5,6), to prophets (for instance, Isaiah 53)?

• Who revealed the messianic hope to Israel, and who in the first century was expecting the Messiah? Consider Luke 1:30-33, John 1:45, John 4:24-26, Luke 24:25-27, 45-47.

Think:

• As you mull over the human predicament, when does being "finite" most frustrate you?

• When do you feel most estranged from people or God? What has raised hope in you?

Digest:

1. To what lengths did God go to scale down to our size in the incarnation? Consider John 1:1,14, I John 1:1-3, John 17:1-5,11,24, and Philippians 2:5-9.

2. How innovative do you think God has been in getting His message to humanity?

3. How would you answer someone who asks, "Why God doesn't just *make* people accept Him?"

Apply:

• When did you begin to respond to God? What most helped you get His message?

• Jews and Gentiles have suffered serious tensions historically, and still do now. Both are in the midst of a profound drama that God has set in motion. Do you resonate at this point with "the Root and the Branch" (Jewish and Gentile believers) being united in the "Remnant" (the messianic community)?

> Lord if the messianic hope has a real basis, how do you want me to respond? Why am I doing this study, from your viewpoint? Show me how to cooperate with you. May you use our group's fellowship to sharpen and edify each other, that we be blessed, and you be pleased.

> Focus: *The identity of this mysterious person who arrives on earth.* God loves us, and has planned our rescue.

A javelin of light stabbed down into the world's time line

Search:
• Who is "the Word"? John 1:1,14
• Who spoke of the Messiah, according to Jesus? Luke 24:25b-27
• Why is the messianic Son superior to all prior revelation? Hebrews 1:1-6
• How all-encompassing is the identity of the Messiah? Revelation 22:13

Think:
•Who puts Jesus forth as "the anointed (i.e. messiah) Son," "the Christ"? Luke 1:30-33, Luke 3:21,22, Luke 9:29-36, Luke 24:25b-27, I John 5:5,6.
• What kind of astounding claims did Jesus make for Himself? John 6:48, John 8:12, 58, John 9:5, John 10 :11, John 11:25-26

Digest:
1. In a Jewish court the testimony of two stood. What are the Father's and the Holy Spirit's testimonies in regard to the Son? Matthew 3:16-17 at His baptism, Mark 9:6-7 at the Transfiguration, John 12:27-32 before the cross.
2. What is His testimony to Himself? Consider Jesus' argument with Jewish leadership: John 7:14-18, John 8:12-59.

Apply:
• What particular evidences of the identity of Jesus have you accepted or rejected?
• What is your main "proof," or reasonable argument, to back up your stance on Jesus?

> Oh Father, I want to be willing to fully embrace your supreme Messenger to the human race. I cannot rightly identify who the Messiah is without revelation from your Spirit. Give me the courage to be willing to receive your illumination – for my sake, and for yours, oh Lord.

The "hour glass" of "headship"

Search:
• What is the meaning of the Fall, as it was experienced? Genesis 2:15-17, Genesis 3:1-24
• What is the meaning of the Fall "reversed"? Romans 5:12-21, Romans 8:1-4, 1 Corinthians 15:22, 45-47

Think:
• What does being "in Adam" by physical birth bring upon us? Genesis 2:15-17, 1 Corinthians. 15:21, 22
• What does being "in Christ" by rebirth give to us? 1 Corinthians 15:22, 45-57, Ephesians 1:3-7, II Peter 1:4

Digest:
1. If you had been Adam or Eve, how would you have reacted to your first sight of death, and your second?
2. When did you experience your first inkling of Christ's life, "the divine nature," actually being present within you?

Apply:
• How do you experience being "in Adam" or "in Christ," in a daily way?
• What does being "accepted in the Beloved" mean to you, down deep within?

Oh Father, I barely realize the seriousness of what being caught "in" my ancestor Adam's line means. I barely grasp the mighty work your Son did in transferring one in Adam into the restored Life you planned for humanity. Awaken me! Transform me according to your passionate desire to see me come into my full inheritance of being included *in* your Son!

The Son's bride

Focus: *The mystery of God's eternal purpose.* God's future for the Son will mean more to us than we could have imagined.

Search:
• What did the Spirit reveal about the messianic Son through David? Psalm 2:7
• Who identified Jesus at the Jordan River? Can we trust the Identifier? Matthew 3:17
• Who ignored the destined wedding of the King's son? Matthew 22:1-10
• When will eternity's Marriage Feast take place? Who will be there? Matthew 25:10-13

Think:
• In whose image, like a child from a father, is Man (male/female)? Genesis 5:1,2
• What is the Creator's purpose for man? Ephesians 1:5-10, 12
• Once the Son accomplished the redemption of man, caring for the negative of sin, what is the positive result He means to move on to accomplish? Galatians 4:4-7

Digest:
1. Who does the scripture call Jesus at His arrival? Luke 1:31-33
2. How is the Messiah understood by the Messianic community after His resurrection? Hebrews 1:1-5
3. Reading back from Revelation, what has the Father been preparing for the Son throughout all these ages? Ephesians 5:25-28, Ephesians 2:4-7, Revelation 21:9a, 22:1,17

Apply:
• When were you made aware of entering into the Beloved, the "Bride"?
• Do you expect to be present at the Marriage Feast of the Lamb?

Oh Father, help me understand what it means to you that I am "accepted in the Beloved." Open my eyes to realize my destiny as one within the Church, the Bride of Christ. Give me a glimpse of the glorious future you have planned for your Son and His wife, that I may more deeply value what He has done to prepare His bride, and look forward worthily to the magnificent future you long to finally bring to fruition.

Focus: *Abraham's experience of covenant with God.* God used the covenant repeatedly throughout both testaments to bond with and teach His people.

The Messianic Seed
(the promised Son)

Search:
• See Abraham's covenant experiences with God recorded in Genesis, the "seed-bed" of the Bible: (Note preplanted clues in key words such as: son, seed, offspring.)
Promise of blessing to all through Abraham, Genesis 12:1-3
Covenant ceremony, prophecy of captivity, Genesis 15:13-21
Circumcision given, sign of the covenant, Genesis 17:1-14
Substitute of the ram for Isaac, sign of the covenant, Genesis 22:1-19
• Look at fulfillments tied to Abraham when the Messiah arrived:
Abraham in Zacharias' prophecy, Luke 1:67-79
Abraham in Mary's Magnificat, Luke 1:54-55
Abraham in the parable about the rich man and Lazarus, Luke 16:19-31

Think:
• How does Abraham tie to "the Messianic hope" in the Old Testament?
The line of promise clarified, Genesis 21:12
God's preview of substitutionary atonement, Genesis 22:1-5
Tracing history from Abraham forward, Psalm 105:3-15, 42
Lamb to the slaughter, Isaiah 53:7-11
• How does Abraham tie to the Messiah's fulfillments in the New Testament?
Jesus identifies who are true descendants of Abraham, John 8:33, 37-40
Jesus' shocking claim: "Before Abraham, I AM," John 8:55-58
Peter's appeal to Israel based on the Abrahamic Covenant, Acts 3:25
If you are Christ's then you are Abraham's offspring! Galatians 3:23-29
Abraham and Melchizedek, foretype of the Great High Priest, Hebrews 7:1-22
Abraham, Isaac, and the resurrection, Hebrews 11:17-19
Abraham, father of all who are justified by faith, Romans 4:1-12

Digest:
1. In what ways did Jesus qualify to contend for the title of "the promised seed of Abraham," the Messiah?
2. What does the resurrection have to do with Jesus being accepted as the Promised One through whom the world would be blessed?

Apply:
• When or how did you realize your heirship – becoming a son/daughter of Abraham?
• Do you expect to sit at the table in the Kingdom with Abraham, Isaac, and Jacob? Why?

Oh Father, reveal to me the mystery of your covenant with Abraham's "seed"! If being included in the "line of promise" decides an individual's destiny, show me how to be in that line, and to do so faithfully. Use me to multiply understanding of that promise!

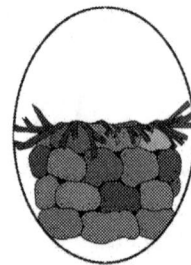

The sacrifice on
Mt. Moriah

Focus: *Profound parallels.* The sacrifices of sons (Abraham's and God's) on Mt. Moriah, were 2000 years apart. "On the mount of the LORD it shall be provided." (Genesis 22:14) Both were resurrected, one in foretype, one in reality.

Search:
• The mysterious drama on Mt. Moriah is told in Genesis 22:1-18. From Abraham's until David's time, some 900 years, "the place the Lord your God shall choose" (for the Temple to replace the Tabernacle) was not revealed. (See Deuteronomy 12:5, 16:2, 6, I Chronicles 21:18-22:1, 23:25.) Jesus said, "Abraham rejoiced to see my day." His resurrection? See John 8:31-59, especially verse 56. Divine testimony to Abraham's faith in God is recorded in Hebrews 11:8-19. The principle of "reckoned righteousness" in Abraham's life is appealed to in Romans 4:3, James 2:21-24.

Think:
• Why do you think God required this of Abraham? Consider Genesis 22:11-18, trying to discern the significance of what God planned and knew about Abraham, the ram, "on the mount of the LORD it shall be provided," and "by your descendants shall all the nations of the earth bless themselves."
• Why do you think Abraham was able to take action on Mt. Moriah in obedience to God's command? Consider Hebrews 11:17-19.
• What was the crux of the Israelites' failure to receive their Messiah, according to Paul's understanding? See Romans 9:30-10:4, Romans 4:20-5:2.

Digest:
1. Trying to empathize with the fathers and sons on Mt. Moriah, what do you think might have been in the hearts of Abraham, of God, of Isaac, of the Messianic Son?
2. What relationship do you see between the two occasions on Mt. Moriah, and the messianic prophecy in Isaiah 52:13-53:12 (especially verses 10,11)?
3. How might these connections strengthen the bedrock of your faith?

Apply:
• Whose righteousness do you count on for your own acceptance with God?
• Have you ever felt you were asked to "slay your Isaac"? What was the result?

Oh Father, like Israel, I too find my pride to be a stumbling block. You have profoundly demonstrated where righteousness comes from, and your longing to impute that righteousness to me. Help me to grasp both how you see my poor "works of righteousness" and your Son's perfect righteousness. Deliver me from false confidence in my own, and teach me to rest in His, in whose Name I come to you.

The Passover in Egypt

Focus: *The Passover, redemption's fore-type, God's basic "redemptive analogy."* The Exodus event lays the foundation for understanding protection from death by the blood of the lamb, and deliverance from slavery. The Passover finds its fulfillment in the Lamb of God's final sacrifice, including deliverance from the bondage of sin.

Search:
• See the Abrahamic covenant renewed with Israel at Mt. Sinai, (Exodus 6:2-5, Exodus 34)
• The Exodus story (amplified by Leviticus, Numbers, Deuteronomy) reveals five foundation stones for God's communication to Israel: The Deliverer, the Deliverance, the Law, the Tabernacle, and the Feasts.
• Preplanted clues made John the Baptist's announcement of the Messiah immediately perceivable to the Jewish community, steeped in the Old Testament. (John 1:29)

Think:
• Do you find helpful G. Campbell Morgan's summary of the Old Testament as: "a sigh for a priest, a quest for a prophet and a cry for a king"?
• How were Moses' and Christ's lives and mediating roles similar? Different? Consider their childhood; reception, mediation, character, burials, destinies, and their identities.
• Note the respect and authority Jesus attributes to Moses: (Matthew 4:1-11, quoting Moses); (Mark 10:3, appealing to Moses); (Matthew 23:2-4, about Moses' seat); (Luke 24:27, Moses' prophetic testimony to the Messiah).
• Note that Moses spoke *for* God, while the Messiah spoke *as* God. How does the book of Hebrews compare the two? (See Hebrews 3:1-6.)

Digest:
1. What can we learn about Jesus and about Moses from their conference on the Mt. of Transfiguration? (Refer to Luke 9:29-31, Matthew 17:1-8, Mark 9:2-8, and II Peter 1:7-18.)
2. Are you willing to accept the testimony of Moses and the prophets according to the Messiah's interpretation? (Consider Luke 24:25-27.)

Apply:
• Seeing how Israel was taught to make God's redemptive analogy indelible in their family life, how do WE do it, or might we do it today?
• What difference would it make?

Oh Father, we stand chided by Jesus' words at Emmaus. We pray that you teach us to search for His presence throughout the Old Testament scriptures, that we may worship Him more fully, and more deeply grasp the fulfillments of the New. We ask in the name of Jesus, with all that His name includes. Amen.

Section IV The Messiah and Moses
    Chapter 8 The Covenants of Law and Grace

Mt. Sinai and Mt. Moriah, "types" of Law and Grace

Focus: *The purpose of "the law."* The law takes us by the hand, shows us our need, and leads us to desire grace.

Search:
• The law given on Mt. Sinai reveals God's holiness and man's need. The *moral* law (Exodus 20:3-17 - The Ten Commandments) is a guide for life-enhancing relationships with God and between people. It provides humanity with a protective moral and legal framework. The *ceremonial* law provides for the offender. God longs for all to be "well" with His children! (Deuteronomy 5:29)
• The need for a new covenant was foreseen and predicted (Jeremiah 31:31-33, quoted in Hebrews 8:8-12, and the whole chapter). Through the Messiah, God's graciousness is fulfilled in history. (Matthew 5:17) Christ's life fulfills the covenant of the law, and His death made the final sacrifice. (Hebrews 10:1-10)
• Two mountains typify the covenants of law and grace. (Hebrews 12:18-24, Galatians 4:24-31, John 1:17) We would not know our need for the second mountain, Mt. Calvary, had we not been enlightened by the first, smoking Mt. Sinai. (Hebrews 8:8-13) The law reveals the sinfulness of sin. "Its straight edge shows us how crooked we are." (Romans 3:20, 7:13) The Holy Spirit introduces a fresh principle working among God's people in this age of grace. Through the indwelling life of the Christ who fulfills the law in us, our loving God has transferred us from the state of "slaves" to "sons" crying "Abba, father!" (Galatians 4:1-7) To embrace "grace" is to find acceptance into God's unconditional love as His own child. Grace is ours only in and through God's gift of the imputed righteousness of Christ. Splendid news! The Spirit of life in Christ Jesus makes free from the law of sin and death. (Romans 8:1-4)

Think:
• What would happen to humanity if society reworded the Ten Commandments, reversing them? Can we see this very thing happening – healthy relationships being smashed, society committing suicide?
• How did the new relationship with God (based on the completed work of the Messiah) become visible the day of the cross, right in the Temple? (Matthew 27:51)

Digest:
1. Israel failed to claim "the righteousness that is by faith," Paul says in Romans 10:4. Is the Church tempted to do the same?
2. Even as a Christian, are you tempted to prefer "law" – the security of legalism to the freedom and responsibility of "grace"?

Apply:
• Do you find yourself giving up because you're not able to keep the law, or taking pride in relative success in keeping it? Do you find either of these responses to be spiritually healthy?
• Do you long to live in the fullness of the new principle of "the Spirit of life in Christ Jesus" to overcome the old "law of sin and death" at work in yourself?

Oh Father...Abba...how we thank you for adopting us into your family, making us sons and daughters! How beyond "good" is your good news for us, how absolutely marvelous to be destined "to be conformed to the image of your Son!"

Section V The Messiah and the Tabernacle
    Chapter 9 The Tabernacle: God's Provided Way of
    Acceptance

Focus: *The Mercy Seat.* The focus of over 50 chapters of the Bible, the Tabernacle served as a bridge between God's austere distance from unholy humanity after the Fall to His closeness since the Messiah has come to "tabernacle among us" and now make us "temples of the Holy Spirit."

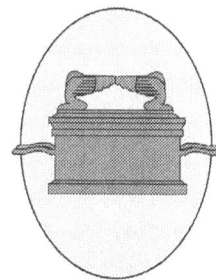

The Ark of the Covenant

Search:
• Explore the plan of the Tabernacle that God gave to Moses "exactly according to the pattern" in Exodus 25-40, with amplification in Leviticus, Numbers, and Deuteronomy.
• In the books of I and II Samuel, I Kings, and I Chronicles, see how the same way of approaching God is continued over 1500 years. The moveable Tabernacle was replaced by a stationary Temple during King Solomon's time. After the Lamb's perfect sacrifice, the sacrificial system carried out in the Temple ended when the Temple was destroyed in 70 AD.
• Notice the continual anchoring of the New Testament message to the Tabernacle. Consider events in the Gospels, applications of the Messiah's life and death to "tabernacle" meanings in the Epistles, His fulfillment of the sacrificial system presented in the book of Hebrews, and images of the Temple throughout Revelation.

Think:
• What function does the Tabernacle serve in God's relationship with His people?
• To what do the "patterns" or "copies" spoken of in Hebrews 9:22-28 refer?
• What is the function of each of the seven pieces of furniture used in the Tabernacle, as described in Exodus?
• Call to mind Christ's claims for these seven symbolic aspects of approach to God being fulfilled in Him, during His incarnational visit.

Digest:
1. How could you use the Tabernacle to present the good news of God's acceptance to a seeker?
2. What is crucial about the order of the seven articles? Their arrangement? Their meanings?

Apply:
• As you present yourself before God, how do you personally participate in the meanings represented by each of these seven symbols?

Oh Father, thank you for showing me how you bridged the gap between your holiness and man's sinfulness. Thank you for giving me a way of approach to you through the Son who you sent to "tabernacle among us." Thank you for splitting the veil when your Perfect Lamb was slain, forever opening the way into your Presence. Enable me to fulfill my role as "a priest unto God" showing others that way. In the Name of the Lamb, Amen.

"Better"

The New Covenant

> Focus: *New covenant: "better"*! God used the Tabernacle and the Temple to house His manifested Presence on earth. At the arrival of the Messiah, God moved His invested Presence from a building in space to a life in time, from the Temple to His Incarnate Son. Christ's life, death, and resurrection progressively parallel and fulfill the function of the Tabernacle. The book of Hebrews explains that this is a far "better" covenant.

Search:

• Examine the book of Hebrews. Its key word is "better." God opened the way for a *better* relationship as a result of the *fulfillment* of the sacrificial system in *Yeshua*.

• Study Hebrews with double vision, seeing how all the elements of the Old Testament Tabernacle are presented as fulfilled now by the Messiah, in the age of the New Covenant.

• Consider Jesus' cry, "It is finished," in the light of your Great High Priest's mighty act of entering the Holy of Holies bearing His own blood, once for all. (Hebrews 9:24-28)

Think:

In the book of Hebrews…

• Consider the brazen altar. How has Christ provided *a better sacrifice*? Hebrews 9:22-26

• Consider the laver. How has He provided *a better sanctification*? Hebrews 10: 10-14

• Consider the Holy Place. How is the Messiah a *better priest*, based upon a *better priesthood*? Hebrews 4:15, 16, 5:6-10, 7:9-17

• How has "the priest after the order of Melchizedek" fulfilled the three symbols in the Holy Place? Consider the bread, the lampstand, the altar of incense, as seen in John 6:45-51, 8:12, 17:1-26.

• How has the Lamb of God provided *better blood* on the Mercy Seat, providing a *better result*? Hebrews 9:11-14, 25-28, 9:15, 10:12-18

• At what significant moment did God signal that *better blood* had been presented, when the Temple's veil was ripped open? Mark 15:38, Hebrews 10:19-22

Digest:

1. How does God's Tabernacle clarify the experience of coming into His fellowship? Fix in your mind the "S" steps: Seeker, Sacrifice, Sanctification, Service, and Satisfaction. Imagine yourself at the one gate, at the altar, at the laver, in the Holy Place, and at the Mercy Seat.

2. How might we see the Tabernacle as an outline – or progression – for the believer's on-going worship?

Apply:

• As you repeatedly come to God, how do you personally participate in the meanings represented by each of these steps from "Seeker" to "Satisfaction"? Who is satisfied?

Oh Father, I thank you that my Savior, our Great High Priest, came forth from the grave, assuring us of the outcome of our faith. "He is risen!" May I "love his appearing" as I await the day when He will "appear the second time" – coming forth from "the sanctuary not made with hands." Meanwhile, enable me to grow into the spirit of Paul's prayer in Philippians 3:8-10, "that I may know him and the power of His resurrection." In His mighty Name, Amen.

Code
7

God's time signature indicating completion: 7

Focus: *The meaning of time*. Jewish scholar Abraham Heschel calls Judaism a religion of time – aiming at the sanctification of time. The Sabbaths are "God's cathedrals in *time*"! Creation was celebrated weekly, and the seven feasts provided yearly for every generation to be exposed to the Tabernacle/Temple's portrayals in *space*.

Search:
• Note sabbath commands, principles, and promises found in Exodus 20:8-11, 16:22-30, and Leviticus 25. Become familiar with the seven appointed "feasts of the Lord" in Leviticus 23.
• What are some of the patterns discernible in God's use of time? Consider the cycles God set up on the basis of 7's: creation, the week, the yearly feast cycle, the 7 x 7 + 1 Jubilee Year, etc.
• The fulfillments accomplished by the Messiah serve as God's "time-markers" as He moves us toward the goal of history. (Ephesians 1:9,10, 3:8-11) Notice the progressive nature of the 7 feasts, seeing something of their eschatological significance, that is, related to last or final things.

Think:
• Time is a great mystery. God gives us hints of Time's origin, its purpose, its essence, its clues. What does God communicate through the repetition of numbers in the scriptures, like 40 days/years, or 7 days/week/years?
• What striking chastisement demonstrated God's holding Israel responsible for keeping the sabbaths of the land? Tie together Ezekiel 20, Jeremiah 25:8-13, 29:10-14, and Daniel 9.
• What does it mean for Jesus to have claimed to be "the Lord of the Sabbath"? Matthew 12:6-8 (quoting Hosea 6:6) Mark 2:28, Luke 6:1-11.

Digest:
1. Hebrews 4:9 says, "So then, there remains a *sabbath rest* for the people of God." What do you think is meant? See the context in Hebrews 4:1-13.
2. Do you sense any personal needs related to the principles of the sabbath, or of spiritual rest?

Apply:
• Some feasts are "completed" by the Messiah, some not. Where do you think history is today in that progression?
• How are you participating in the process after the 4th feast, the middle one, *Shavuot* (Pentecost)?

Oh Father, thank you for the Sabbath rest you have provided. Awaken me to the clues to history which you have given! May I "watch" in kinship with your passion to complete your marvelous plan. In the Name of your Son, Lord of the Sabbath, Amen.

Section VI The Messiah and the Feasts
Chapter 12 The Feasts of God's Year and of Eternity

The Feasts

Focus: *The Feasts unto the Lord.* God taught His people crucial meanings through dramatic celebrations repeated three seasons of each year in the "theater" of the Temple in Jerusalem. These dramas transfer into the New Testament powerfully.

Search:
• Be familiar with the seven appointed feasts of the Lord, first introduced in Exodus 23:14-17, and found in Leviticus 23, Numbers 28, 29, Deuteronomy 16, and the Jubilee Year in Leviticus 25.

• For basic biblical understanding, it is important to learn the timing of the feasts (the cycles of the agricultural year) and their calendar (lunar, not solar). Imbedded in the feasts we find God's key principles of cultural and spiritual practice.

• Take note of God's use of the feasts as a platform for His message, such as Passover in Joshua 5, the Feast of Tabernacles in Ezra 3:1-6 and Nehemiah 8 and 9. Notice Christ's use of dramatic moments in the feast ceremonies, such as in the Feast of Tabernacles in John 7 and 8, God's use of the Passover for the sacrifice of the final Lamb of God, the Messiah's resurrection on First Fruits, the Spirit's use of the Feast of Weeks (Pentecost) in Acts 2, and many more.

• Unlike cyclical views of existence, the God of Abraham reveals history to be linear, moving toward a goal. See promises to Israel in Genesis and Exodus, to the Church in Ephesians 1:9,10, 3:8-11. The progressive nature of the 7 feasts helps us sense something of their eschatological significance, like the drama of the ages being played out in 7 acts.

Think:
• What clues to the identity of the Messiah are found in the Spring Feast triad - Passover (*Pesach*), Unleavened Bread, and First Fruits?

• What seems to be the "typological" meaning of the middle feast season, the Feast of Weeks (*Shavuot*) in the summer harvest period, called Pentecost in Greek?

• Do the three Fall Feasts appear to have been "fulfilled" yet? i.e. Trumpets (*Rosh Hoshana*), Day of Atonement (*Yom Kippur*), and Tabernacles or Booths (*Sukkot*)? What does the "8th Day" in Leviticus 23:39 signify? In what sense does the High Priest's emergence from the Holy of Holies on the Day of Atonement still await fulfillment? See Hebrews 9:24,28.

Digest:
1. Where do you see our world today, along God's progression toward the climax of history?

2. What role are you playing in the spiritual completion of *Shavuot*, the Summer Feast initiating harvest time?

3. With what emotions, hopes, or dreads, do you anticipate the spiritual completion of the Fall Feasts in the Messiah's ingathering and Second Coming?

Apply:
• With what passion do you suppose the Messiah wants His Bride to participate in present and future feasts? i.e. in His personal feast with a believer shown by Revelation 3:20, or in the Church's communal feast with Him through the Lord's Supper; or in the future Marriage Feast of the Lamb, previewed in Revelation 19:6-9?

Lover of my soul, give me a passion to pore over your love-letter, reading between the lines with deepening insight and holy anticipation. The Spirit and the Bride say, "Come Lord Jesus!" Yes! Amen

Shepherd's staff,
with cross

> Focus: *The root and offspring of David.* Dr. G. Campbell Morgan sees the Old Testament as "a sigh for the priest, a quest for the prophet, and a cry for the king." When Israel cried for a king, the lives of the Monarchy's kings Saul, David, and Solomon became object lessons packed with practical meaning and imbedded with eschatological promises.

Search:

• Trace the movement from Samuel's leadership as a prophet, to Israel's demand for a king and that outworking, in I and II Samuel, I and II Kings, I and II Chronicles.

• God calls David "a man after my own heart." David's heart is revealed by his shepherd attitude (Psalm 23, II Samuel 5:2, 12:1-14); his Jonathan/David friendship (I Samuel 18:1-3, 20:8, 23:15-18, II Samuel 1:11-25); his respect for "the Lord's anointed" (I Samuel 24:6, 26:22,23); his honest confession (Psalm 32,51) and passion for God (II Samuel 7:18-28, Psalm 62,63,139,142).

• Search the Psalms for attitudes toward God's Kingship and for prophetic utterances related to the Messianic King. Especially see Psalm 2, and 110. Notice how steeped Jesus was in the Psalms of His forefather, David, quoting the Psalms as evidence of His own identity (Psalm 2, Psalm 110 repeatedly quoted in the New Testament). Jesus cried out the opening line of David's Psalm 22 at the cross.

Think:

• How was God's early history with Israel expressed as a spiritual theocracy rather than in the monarchical forms of Gentile nations?

• Who was really the King of Israel? Did David understand that?

• What parallels do you find between David and Christ? Consider their hearts, their histories, their eschatological connection, and their genealogical line recorded in Matthew 1:1, Luke 1: 68,69, 2:4.

Digest:

1. What promises to David have been fulfilled, and which remain unfulfilled? See II Samuel 7:8-17, Luke 1:32,33, Revelation 22:16.
2. What stake do we today have in that fulfillment?

Apply:

• How earnestly do I desire to be "a man (or woman) after God's own heart"?

• Have I purposely made the King of kings my own sovereign and Lord? If I have, how does that substantially change my life?

Oh Lord, search my heart, try me, cleanse me. May your Spirit reveal your shepherd Kingship to me. Show me the identity of the Royal Son in His majesty, that I may worship and adore Him, the very One who even now brings my cry to your throne.

Crown

Focus: *The Messianic King.* God's Royal Son came first as the Suffering Servant to reverse the cosmic catastrophe of the Fall. God promises He will come to rule as King at His second advent, between which His royal Bride is being gathered and prepared, since she, too, wonder of wonders, is destined for the Throne!

Search:

• Popular expectations surfaced repeatedly – of the coming King (John 1:45, Matthew 2:2) and "Son of David" (Matthew 12:23,21:9). Surely Jesus demonstrated divine power – over matter (John 2:1-11, 6:16-21), over nature (Matthew 8:23-27), over evil (Mark 5:1-20), over sickness (Matthew 4:23,24, 9:35,36, 12:22,23, John 9:1-7), and over death (Luke 7:11-17, Mark 5:35-43, John 11:1-44).

• Jesus attested to His foretold kingship openly, calling Himself "greater than David's son, Solomon" (Matthew 12:42), applying prophetic passages about the Royal Son to Himself (Psalm 2, 110), and claiming pre-existence even before Abraham (John 8:56-58), to whom the seed to bless all nations was promised.

• Although Jesus' power and popularity were enough for Him to seize the kingship, He made it clear that the Son of Man had come in the flesh for the express purpose of dying (Mark 10:45, John 10:15-18, Matthew 16:21, Mark 8:30-32, 9:31, Matthew 20:17-19, 26:2). He warned that His mission would be rejected (Matthew 21:37-45) although He was acclaimed as the Son of David the very week of His crucifixion (Matthew 21:4-17).

• The Messiah's kingship, beyond Israel's ken, was announced in heaven (Revelation 11:15). He gave clues on earth about His kinship and kingdom repeatedly through parables and analogies promising fulfillment. See Matthew 13:45,46, 21:33-43, 22:1-14, 25:1-13, 25:31-46 for examples.

• We are to await events in the future: His coming in full Messianic kingship (Revelation 11:15-18, 19:11-16), the marriage feast of the Lamb (Revelation 19:6-9), and the bowing of every knee (Philippians 2:9-11).

Think:

• What deeper meanings of Christ's mission has the Holy Spirit continued to teach the messianic community, after His departure? Full "good news" climaxes in post-Pentecost insights given by God the Holy Spirit, as in Philippians 2:5-11, Colossians 1:11-20, I Timothy 1:15-17, 6:13-16, Hebrews 9:27, 28, and the worship scenes of Revelation 4:9-5:14, 11:15, 21:22-26.

Digest:

1. Now that both Old and New Testament insights into the Messianic Kingdom have been given to us, how authentically am I conforming my life to the fullness of Christ's kingship, or the Godhead's revelation of the scope and destiny of the Kingdom?

Apply:

• What do I expect my identification with this King to cost me . . . or reward me?

Yes Lord Jesus, I Timothy 1:17, "To the King of the ages, immortal, invisible, the only God, be honor and glory for ever and ever! Amen"!

SectionVIII The Messiah and the Prophets
Chapter 15 Prophets and Prophecies in the Old Testament

"The Elijah"

Focus: *Messiah, the ultimate Prophet.* The Hebrews did not deify their kings; in fact, their prophets served like "checks and balances" to kings and priests. God's messages given by His prophets throughout history provide a means of corroborating His stated will, His judgments, and His reliability.

Search:

• Early chapters of the Messiah Mystery focused on Moses, key prophet for his times. See Genesis through Deuteronomy. In the historical books, oral prophecies are recorded from men like Nathan during the United Kingdom, and Elijah and Elisha during the Divided Kingdom. (See I and II Samuel, Kings, and Chronicles.)

• Eventually the written prophetic books come on the scene, know as "the Major and Minor Prophets" (i.e. long or short). They record Israel's and Judah's struggles during their decline and fall, exile, and Judah's return. The prophetic books overlap each other, as various prophets speak for God during the period of the Divided Kingdom's few good and many evil kings.

• Malachi speaks the last prophetic words in the Old Testament, before a 400 year silence for the writing prophets.

• Matthew begins where Malachi left off, with the prophet John the Baptist tied to Malachi. This Forerunner (who Jesus identifies as "the Elijah" in Matthew 11:10,11) points to the ultimate Prophet, God's Messiah, who fulfills the Old Testament messianic prophecies and speaks not *for* but *as* God. Many of Christ's prophecies regarding Himself and Israel take place between 30 and 70 AD. God's people await the fulfillment of yet future promises with confidence. (See the Gospels and Revelation.)

Think:

• What was the relationship between Hebrew kings and prophets, and between prophets and priests?

• To what various time periods may a prophecy refer?

• What were the major themes of Old Testament prophetic messages?

• What was the Hebrews' most typical response to their prophets? See Matthew 23:29-39, Acts 7:51-53.

Digest:

1. Had you been called to be a prophet, what kind of difficulties could you envision?

2. As you read of God's agony over His people, do you ever have a sense of sharing in the pathos of God?

Apply:

• What prophetic fulfillment means the most to you?

• What promises of God recorded through the prophets are you counting upon still in the future?

Lord, tune my heart and life to you! Teach me how you evaluate, how surely you judge. Raise my eyes and hopes to meet your promises – for now, and for eternity. Through the Alpha and Omega, Amen.

Focus: *Prophetic authenticity.* Jesus perfectly hits the seven bull's eye circles of prophetic authenticity that could be used for identifying the Messiah. Moving from general to specific, Christ fulfills every circle, narrowing the candidates who could qualify down to the only possible One!

A bull's eye

Search:

• Trace the "Elijah" tie between the last prophet's prophecies and the introduction to the New Testament. (Malachi 4:4-6 related to Luke 1:16,17 and Malachi 3:1 related to Luke 7:26,27)

• Prophecy specified the Messiah's humanity (Genesis 3:15), Jewishness (Genesis 12:1-3, 28:10-15), tribe (Genesis 49:10), birthplace (Micah 5:2), His reception and death (Isaiah 52:13-53:12), the timing of His appearance (Daniel 9:24-26). Who qualifies?

• Consider the details of the life and death of Jesus prophesied in the Suffering Servant passage, Isaiah 52:13-53:12. Our precedent for applying this passage to Jesus comes from His own application of it to Himself in Luke 22:37, and the Apostles' applying it to Him, for instance in John 12:38, Acts 8:32. Like Psalm 2, Psalm 110:1 is repeatedly quoted in the New Testament as the messianic reference to God's Son. Grasp its importantance to Jesus in Mark 12:36, and to Peter in Acts 2:34,35. Melchizedek appears in Genesis 14, and is referred to repeatedly in Hebrews. (5:5-10, 6:19, 20, 7:11-15) See how the Spirit uses Melchizedek as the precedent to authenticate Jesus' high priesthood.

Think:

• What is the tie between Moses and Jesus as prophets? See Deuteronomy 18:15-19, Acts 3:21-24.

• How was Jesus different from other prophets?

• How accurate were Jesus' prophetic insights - into Israel's rejection of the Son, the timing of His own death, Hhis disciples' defection, His resurrection, the destruction of the Temple?

• What prophecies uttered by the Son help us assess His reliability, or His intentions?

Digest:

1. Which group are you in, as you consider Jesus' prophetic parable of the ten virgins?

2. What do you expect to happen to you when Christ enacts His predicted role as judge?

Apply:

What warnings from *Jesus the prophet* do you take most seriously?

What specific hopes engendered by Christ's promises are you counting upon?

Almighty God who knows the end from the beginning, build in me a grasp of the prophetic clues to the mystery of your plan woven throughout history. Open my eyes to the emerging revelation of your Son's identity. Reinforce my confidence in your purposes and in the Messiah's prophetic role in your mighty plan, that I may worship rightly, and live rightly in your sight.

Emmanuel

Focus: *The Incarnation.* Turning now from the fore-shadowing of the Old Testament, we are faced with Emmanuel, "God with us," tabernacling with us in the flesh. Isaiah 7:14, Matthew 1:23.

Search:
• Digest the four witnesses to the life of Jesus in the four Gospels. They were written by the eye-witness disciples, Matthew and John; by Dr. Luke, who traveled with Paul; and by Peter's nephew, Mark.
• Notice the synoptic gospels' parallels, and the additional window provided by John, who included more of Jesus' ministry in Judea. Note the concentration of the Gospels on the week of His shocking crucifixion and astounding resurrection.
• Study a random sample of the God-man's life. Picture Jesus as if you were traveling with Him for a couple of days, by staying with Him, say, through Matthew 9 and 10.

Think:
• God is allowing us to see Him now "in the face of His Son." Jesus provides three windows through which we may sight Him. He claims to show us *God's character* (John 14:9), *God's mind* (John 8:28, 7:16,17) and *God's powerful works* (John 14:11)
• We are delighted by Christ's display of *God's character*, His utter love, even His humor. Who of us is loving Him back, enjoying Him? Christ's revolutionary teachings (*God's Mind*) thrill us as we sense His unpretentious wisdom, wholeness, tenderness, and incisiveness. He patiently teaches individuals and groups, pouring forth a wealth of discourses, parables, beatitudes, prayers, dialogues, "I Am's", revelations, warnings, and woes. Not codified, these indispensable guides to life must be mined from the Gospels like gold.
• What do Jesus' miracles signify about the nature of *God's power* and love, and the identity of the One performing them? Recognition of the Messiah's IDENTITY was, and still is, His final test question. See Matthew 16:16, Mark 8:29, Luke 9:20.

Digest:
1. What sort of people were His enemies, and what sort of people were drawn to Him? Significance?
2. If Jesus sat down with you (as with the woman at the well, or at Simon's dinner) what do you think He would say to you? Consider John 4:13-42, Luke 7:36-50.
3. Jesus told people who realized who He was *not* to tell anyone yet. Why? See Matthew 16:9.

Apply:
• Am I enjoying God's character in Jesus?
• Do I earnestly labor to mine gold from God's mind, uncovered in Jesus' teachings?
• How am I answering Jesus' inescapable question: "Who do you say that I am?"

How you have surprised me, Almighty God, revealing yourself in the winsome face of Jesus the Christ! You are full of surprises. I am stumbling into an unimaginably wonderful Kingdom! And yet . . . your Son made it clear that "Who I am cost me my life, and if you embrace me, it can cost you yours too." Almighty Father, God in the Flesh, Spirit of the Living God, live in me. Empower and enable me.

SectionIX The Messiah Manifested
Chapter 18 The Death and Resurrection of Christ

Christ's cross and resurrection

Focus: *The Son's vindication.* Knowing His time was at hand, Jesus' last night with His disciples is packed with meaning. (John 13-17) God the Father's fore-ordained sacrifice of His Son has arrived. His resurrection by the power of the Spirit split history into "before and after" the incarnation. Likewise it splits our personal histories into "before and after" our entrance into the resurrection life of Jesus the Christ.

Search:

• Digest the four witnesses' accounts of the events of Jesus' passion – His Passover supper with His disciples, their desertion, the trials, His crucifixion, and then His totally unexpected resurrection.

• Hear the unrelenting question and varying answers to: "Who is this man?" Compare Matthew 26-28, Mark 14-16, Luke 22-24, and John 13-21. Ask God for spiritual insight to grasp the meaning of the sacrifice of the promised Son or "seed" (Genesis 3:15, Exodus 17) - foreseen in Abraham's and Isaac's experience on Mt. Moriah (Exodus 22), and throughout the sacrifices of the Tabernacle and later the Temple. See Exodus 25-31, 34-40, most of Leviticus, Numbers 7-10, 28, 29, Deuteronomy 14-16.

• The mystery of the cross can only be understood by "the eyes of our understanding being enlightened by the Spirit of God." (Ephesians 1:18) Jesus Himself explained much during His forty post-resurrection days on earth. From heaven, He continued to reveal more depth of meaning through the Holy Spirit's enlightening the disciples and Paul thereafter. These deepening insights will be the focus of Sections X and XI.

Think:

• During the Messiah's passion, what did the rejection mean – not only by men, but seemingly by God Himself? (Mark 15:34, Matthew 27:46, Psalm 22:1)
What was actually signified by the Messiah's gasp, "It is finished!"? (John 19:30)

Digest:

1. What difference does the resurrection make…to our faith in the reliability of Jesus… to us at death?
2. Why is the *resurrection* Paul's central teaching as he carried God's amazing news out to the world?
3. Have you appropriated the benefits of Christ's sacrifice to your own life? That is (according to Watchman Nee's explanation), are you willing to see the *blood* as God sees it, as satisfactory propitiation for the sins of the world? Are you willing to accept the *cross* as you see it, as your own death penalty paid by Christ?

Apply:

• Are you appropriating the saving death of Christ - "the finished work of Christ"?
• Are you appropriating the saving life of Christ - "the power of the resurrection"?

Dear Father, your word tells me that Christ has finished the work of my redemption. It tells me that your Son's resurrection life infused into the believers is our crowning good news. That I need that life, that I want that life, is obvious, but that I *have* life can only be revealed to me by your Spirit. Enlighten the eyes of my understanding that, as Paul prayed, I may know "what is the hope to which you have called me, and what are the riches of your glorious inheritance in the saints …." Amen.

Tongues of fire

Focus: *God's Spirit outpoured.* Curtain time for Act Three in God's great drama of redemption! Suddenly come wind, fire, multi-languages speaking God's mighty works. Jesus of Nazareth, raised up by God and exalted at His right hand, is received by 3,000 from all over the known world, present in Jerusalem by God's design, for the Feast of *Shavuot.* (That fourth feast is translated "the Feast of Weeks" in English, and is known to us today by the Greek word, "Pentecost.")

Search:
• Walk through Acts 2 with the disciples and the crowd. Try to hear, see, smell, feel, and wonder as they might have.
• Ponder Peter's application of Joel 2:28-32 to this shocking miracle found in Acts 2:16-21. With John 7:37-39 as a background, grasp the impact of Acts 2:33.
• Think through Jesus' preparatory teachings about the Holy Spirit, given the night before His crucifixion, especially in John 14:25,26, 15:26, 16:5-15.
• See the continuing presence of the Messiah, in the Person of the Spirit of God, at work in Acts 2:42-47, 3:3-16, 4:7-12, 24-30.

Think:
• Considering what was presented in Section VI on the Feasts of Israel, what do you think about the event at the Feast of *Shavuot,* fifty days after the resurrection? How was that day a fulfillment of the meanings symbolized in the fourth feast? Recall Exodus 34:22, Leviticus 23:15, and Deuteronomy 16:9-12, as the background for this event in Acts 2.
• How was the power of the Holy Spirit manifested, and what were some of the results during the first few weeks after Pentecost? See Acts 2:2-4, 3:1-16; 4:32-35; 5:1-16.

Digest:
1. In John 16:5-15, Christ told the disciples that the Holy Spirit's presence would be "better" than Jesus' bodily presence. Why better for them, why better for the world?
2. What crucial gifts has God the Holy Spirit given to believers?

Apply:
• Do I purposely invite the Spirit to reveal Christ to me? Do I thank Him?
• Do I ever come to the point of awe before the Holy Spirit, realizing He is equally deserving of worship, along with the Son and the Father?

Spirit of God, awaken me to your astounding presence within me since I opened my life to the Messiah! Thank you for interpreting the scriptures to my heart, for revealing my Lord to me, for being "Christ in me, the hope of glory."

God as three in One

Focus: *God's indwelling Spirit*. Ours is called the "age of the Holy Spirit." Actually, the "third Person of the Trinity" is the closest of the Godhead to believers as this time in history.

Search:

• Grasping the *identity* of the Holy Spirit is crucial. He is One with God, the agent of the first creation and the new creation. Trace the unity and diversity of the triune God in passages such as Luke 3:21,22, Mark 9:2-9, Romans 8:9, 11-14, I Corinthians 2:11-14, II Corinthians 3:17, Galatians 4:6, Philippians 1:19, Ephesians 1:13,14, 2:18-22, 3:4-17, Titus 3:5.

• The Holy Spirit has inspired the *scriptures* to be made available to man, and interprets them for us. See II Peter 1:21, I Timothy 1:16-18, II Timothy 3:16.

• Let us appreciate the way God pours His life into His people through the Holy Spirit made available to each and all believers. Being not only our source of scripture, He is also the One who ministers to us in *many roles* as He baptizes (Acts 1:5), indwells (John 14:17), fills (Acts 2:4,9:17,13:52), teaches (I Corinthians 2:6-16), guides (John 16:12-15), convicts (John 16:8-10), gifts (I Corinthians 12:1-11, Ephesians 4:11-16), gives fruit (Galatians 5:16-18), strengthens (Ephesians 3:16), counsels (John 15:26-16:7), comforts (John 14:16 KJV), sanctifies (II Thessalonians 2:13), seals (Ephesians 4:30), unites us (I Corinthians 12:12-27, Ephesians 2:11-21, 4:4), and more!

Think:

• If we had only the Gospels, but not the Spirit's teaching in the Acts and the Letters, what would we be missing? Consider insights such as "living under the law vs. under the Spirit," "the middle wall of partition broken down," "the blessed hope," " the better priesthood," etc.

• Why do you think the word "Trinity" was coined? Do you think it was justified?

Digest:

1. Why do the historical record of Acts and the spiritual teachings of the Letters not seem to lead the church to total uniformity in liturgy? For instance, how do infant baptism and immersion baptism reflect different aspects of biblical history?

Apply:

• What spiritual fruits and gifts do you personally sense to be growing out of your relationship to the indwelling Spirit, or poured out upon you by Him? Rejoice!

Dear Father, thank you for the marvelous gift of your Spirit, and all He does in and through me to glorify your Son. Reveal and multiply His work in me, and throughout the world, to the praise of your glory!

Root and Branches

> Focus: *Every tribe, language, people, and nation.* Far from relegated to the grave, the Messiah is directing history from His exalted throne. That "light to the Gentiles" prophesied by Isaiah is being fulfilled at last. Starting with Israel, the Root, God is grafting in Gentiles, "unnatural branches" as He moves toward the goal which we can glimpse in Revelation 5:9,10.

Search:

• The book of Acts gives a condensed historical record of God's birthing of the New Covenant community, from Jerusalem to Judea to Samaria and out to the Gentile world. Every episode reveals some surprising move, as the Spirit poured out by the Messiah enthroned in heaven, disrupts the status quo on earth.

• Matching Acts with the New Testament letters, we can discern the interwoven histories of the early Christian communities, the Spirit's revelations they received, the miraculous power they saw working within them, and the problems they had to work through.

• The Jerusalem Counsel (Acts 15) profoundly shaped the direction the messianic community took, to which all non-Jewish believers in the Messiah are heirs today. Study their ruling (Acts 15:13-21), based upon prophecy and the overriding indications of the Spirit, to see how guidelines for spiritual, physical, and moral purity were given. Furthermore, close Jew/Gentile fellowship was preserved.

• In Christ, the dividing wall of partition was broken down by God Himself, creating "one new man in Christ" – revolutionary! See Ephesians 2:11-22, Galatians 3:26-29, Philippians 3:2-11. Paul devotes Romans 9-11 to exploring crucial relationships between the Root and the Branches, i.e. Israel and the Gentile believers.

Think:

• What role did persecution play in bursting the geographic and racial boundaries of the messianic community? What role did God's direct intervention play?

• Had the Jerusalem Council decided to require circumcision of Gentile believers, do you think you would be studying the mystery of the Messiah today?

Digest:

1. Since "our redemption draws nigh," what are our responsibility and our privilege during the age of the Spirit – the age of grace – before the close of this age?

2. Christians today can search out history to learn how it happened in the early centuries that messianic Jewish believers were separated from both the Jewish and later the Christian communities. Moving forward, does the legacy of the holocaust, and the tragic situation in the Middle East today, cry out for repentance, healing, and restoration?

Apply:

• What is my commitment to "the full number of Gentiles" coming in? Consider Romans 11:25.

• Do I want to take part in healing the rift among people in the Root and the Branches? How?

Oh Father, you must groan as you see creation still groaning. Work in us the sorrow and anguish Paul carried from your heart to his. Oh that Israel may be saved! O that the full number of Gentiles may be completed! Oh that the creation be liberated from its bondage to decay and be brought into the glorious freedom of the children of God!

"in"

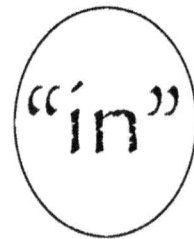

The Gospel's crucial word: "in"

> Focus: *The believer's inclusion.* All that comes to us through receiving Christ is ours because God considers us to be "in Christ." See Ephesians 1:3,4,6,10-13, 3:6,12. This "in-ness" is not only a principle underlying all that is credited to us as God's imputed gift, it is a living fact true of each and every child of God born of His Spirit into the Messiah's community, the Body of Christ. With "in-ness" underlying all of God's explanations of the believer's relationship with Him, the major analogies describing it can best be understood.

Search:
• *The Head directing the body*: Colossians 1:17-20, Ephesians 4:13-16, I Corinthians 12:12-26.
• *The Cornerstone and His living temple*: Psalm 18:22, Isaiah 28:16, Romans 9:33, I Corinthians 6:15-20, Ephesians 2:19-22, Matthew 21:42-44, I Peter 2:4-7, I Corinthians 3:16,19.
• *The Heir and His co-heirs of the Kingdom*: Hebrews 1:2, Ephesians 3:5,6, James 2:5, Colossians 1:11-14.
• *The Sovereign and His ambassadors*: Luke 14:15-24 with John 1:11-13, John 20:21, Mark 16:15, Matthew 28:18-20, II Corinthians 5:17-21.
• *The Commander and His soldiers*: Ephesians 6:10-18, II Timothy 2:1-4.
• *The Bridegroom and His bride*: Ephesians 5:21-32, Revelation 19:6-9, 22:17.

Think:
• How important to God is the believer's "inclusion"? How important to the believer is being "in Christ"?
• What does the Church's being "the body of Christ" mean?
• How do the Old Testament passages about the Tabernacle and Temple help indwelt believers grasp the meaning of actually being temples of the Holy Spirit, themselves?
• What does the spiritual inheritance of being "co-heirs with Christ" include?
• If Christians are soldiers of the King, who is the enemy? How important is it to rightly identify our battlefield?

Digest:
1. Why is the New Testament form for the "temple" fitted for the circumstances of history, since 70 AD?
2. How do you respond to finding the bride and groom love relationship to be the analogy with which we are left at the end of the Bible?

Apply:
• Do you base your assurance and confidence as a Christian on being "in Christ"?
• Which of the six analogies picturing Christ's relationship with His own is most meaningful to you?

Dear Lord, how marvelously you have destined your children! Solidify our confidence in the truth of the "in-ness" which you have chosen to lovingly bestow upon us. Awaken us to the depths of relationship with you that your Spirit has communicated in your word. May you be pleased with lives that reflect the majestic roles you have built into our inclusion! We come to you in the name of our Head, our Cornerstone, our co-Heir, our Sovereign, our Commander, and our Bridegroom.

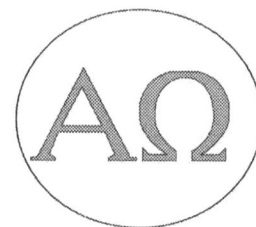

AΩ

The Alpha & Omega

Focus: *Worthy is the Lamb*! The Spirit of God has presented the Messiah pre-figured in the Old Testament. He is fulfilling His role as Seed, Son, Lamb, High Priest, and Suffering Servant in the New Testament. Identity concealed has become identity revealed. But where is the King? At last, the King of kings appears, discloses His full identity (Revelation 22:13) and goes into action. Be encouraged or be warned: know that the Kingdom of God will triumph just as surely as God's promises are true.

Search:
• Behold the King at the heart of the Kingdom in Revelation chapter 1.
• Hear His message to the Church in Revelation 2 and 3.
• See what is happening in Heaven in chapters 4 and 5.
• Glimpse judgment poised, restrained, and awaited in chapters 6 and 7. Note previous warnings in Matthew 21:33-43, 22:1-14, 25:1-13.
• Observe woe to the world, but praise in heaven in chapters 8-16. Face final judgment and resolutions in chapters 17-20. (Note previous descriptions in Matthew 25:31-46, John 5:21-24.)
• Rejoice in the destiny of the faithful remnant, in chapters 21,22.

Think:
• How does Jesus appear in the introductory verses of Revelation? What surrounds Him? What does His garb suggest about the role He is manifesting while He is giving this revelation to John, the one disciple still left alive?
• How would you summarize the major admonitions of the Messiah's letters to the seven churches at the opening of Revelation? What does the number "seven" signify?
• How are heaven and earth contrasted in the central section of Revelation? What is happening in each location? Notice that the Lamb's sacrifice is the center of worship in both realms.
• What new role do we see Jesus manifesting in the latter chapters of Revelation? Why have we not seen Him fully in that role before?
• Why does no drawn-out battle between Good and Evil appear at the climax of the end-time traumas? When was the battle actually fought? See John 12:31,32.
• What do the closing chapters of Revelation reveal about God's ultimate goal?

Digest:
1. What scripture do you think is a good example of the triple application of a prophetic message (i.e. one speaking to a local situation, having a wider application, and yet a future fulfillment)?
2. Why do you think God is justified in saying He is not "ashamed" to be called the God of those who have suffered? (Hebrews 11:16) What is ahead for them?

Apply:
• Do you really think life's struggles are "worth it all" for a believer?
• How much does it matter to you, that the effects of man's on-going disobedience and rebellion be nullified, that right finally triumph, and that God be proved to be *just* as well as loving?

Almighty Father, "Yes!" "Amen!" The Spirit and the Bride say, "Come Lord Jesus!"

The Throne

Focus: *Life's most crucial identities.* "Who" has been the major theme of the Messiah's mystery. The Father wants us to recognize the Messiah's identity, so that we will desire Him. He has also been shaping a second identity, the Bride. The Son promised to return for His Bride, within whom each of us is potentially included. The Bridegroom's love brought redemption to its goal, and it is His love that will lead the way into the marvelous new creation the Bride is destined to share!

Search:

• Revelation is the apocalyptic book. Read quickly through it to get a feel for mysteries glimpsed, without straining to develop dogmatic interpretations of details. Revelation strives to break the conceptualization barrier between heaven and earth, showing us "things to come" in terms human beings can understand, in terms of our five senses. Revelation looks *back from eternity* into time. Matthew 21-25 is called "the little Revelation." When on earth, the Messiah gave glimpses of the happenings found in the Apocalypse, but looking *forward toward eternity.* The supreme Prophet, Jesus, prepares us for life-defining completions both on earth and in heaven.

• Discern from the scripture the second mystery: "Who will make up the Messiah's Bride?" See clearly who will be included in "the remnant." Work through Ephesians 2:11-22, Revelation 5:9,10, 15:4, 19:6-9. Scripture points to our own responsibility to choose or refuse to be included in the Bride. See John 1:10-13, John 3:16, 20, 31, I John 5:9-13.

• We discover that the Bride all along has been destined for the throne! God wooed Israel (Hosea 1-3). The Bible begins and ends with a marriage. The anticipated wedding was already in the Bridegroom's heart when He told the parables in Mark 2:19,20, Matthew 22:2-10. The Spirit reveals more of the mystery in Ephesians 5. In God's eyes, the Bride is already seated in heaven with her exalted Bridegroom. See Ephesians 2:4-7, and Acts 2:33. Revelation shows her there in the final scenes in Revelation 19:8,9. Included in Christ, the Groom's history is now the Bride's history, and her future is also whatever His is to be. This is God's doing, not our own. Amazing grace! Amazing love!

Think:

• Jesus promised, "I am coming soon." "Soon" implies many things: warning, hope, urgency. See how Jesus framed each into His promises, such as in II Corinthians 6:1,2, John 14:1-3, Matthew 25:1-13.

Digest:

1. What does Matthew 24:3-34 (which defines "when") say to me personally, and to believers today? Compared with fallen Adam and Eve, what is to be the destiny of the Second Adam's wife, the Church (Ephesians 2:6, 5:25-27), and the Second Adam, Christ? (I Corinthians 15:21-28, Philippians 2:9-11, Revelation 5:12,13) God assures believers that they are "more than conquerors." (Romans 8:28,29) The Messiah's call to the seven churches promises marvelous rewards to those "who overcome." See Revelation 2:7,11,17, 26, 3:5,12,21.

2. What does it mean to you that those letters end with Jesus begging to be heard and knocking outside the door of the *believer's* heart? (Revelation 3:20)

Apply:

• Can you imagine meeting God's Son face to face, and being among the blessed company of believers from all time when He presents His Bride at the Throne of God?

Hallelujah! "Thus be it!" Yes, "Amen!"

Messiah Mystery Focus Page Response Template
Section:
Chapter:
Name:
Date:

Focus:

Search:

Think:

Digest:

Apply:

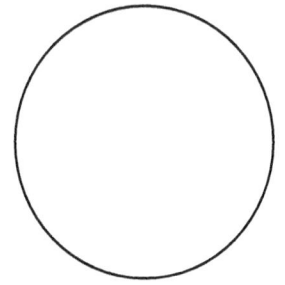

Symbol:

Personal Prayer:

IV. MULTIPLYING YOUR STUDY'S USEFULNESS

This Section's Purpose:
The Messiah Mystery's panoramic form covers such a wide span and variety of biblical history and themes, that the time invested in studying the Genesis-to-Revelation material calls for ways to conserve the material covered for future use. The Layered Teaching File is a method of collecting and filing teaching materials. We are admonished to "teach others who will teach others," as the Spirit encouraged Timothy through his mentor, the Apostle Paul, recorded in II Timothy 2:2. Finally, creative teaching is encouraged, and examples are given.

BUILDING YOUR LAYERED TEACHING FILE

THE SEARCH

The Messiah Mystery essentially studies God's revelation by "systems" some find easier to grasp separately, than by trying to tackle the whole Bible at once. People in medical training study the skeleton, then the organs, followed by various systems such as the digestive system, the nervous system, the muscular system, and finally the skin enveloping the human and making that person a visible entity.

We need to grasp the function of various spiritual systems included in the word of God. Many of them are outlined in Genesis to Deuternomy (the *Torah*, in Hebrew, or the Law), such as man's sin problem, the Abrahamic covenant, the Davidic promises, prophetic predictions, and so on.

When the Messiah appears on earth in the Incarnation, the muscles, skin, eyes, mouth, and touch of the Son of God emerge into the open! We begin to realize just Who we are seeing in the New Testament! He is not a stranger, but a Friend who has revealed Himself with intricate precision throughout the Old Testament's unfolding of God's eternal plan.

After the Messiah's Ascension and Enthronement, the Holy Spirit is poured out. The Letters of the New Testament teach us that believers are in union with Jesus. The Head is at the right hand of the Father; the Body is on earth. The believing community, indwelt by the Spirit of Christ, is being prepared as a bride for the consummation toward which the Heavenly Father's plan has been moving. Thus God reveals glimpses of His plan, from Genesis to Revelation. Our Lord's urgent plea in Revelation is that having eyes we would see, having ears we would hear!

OUR RESPONSE

Who of us is seeing, hearing? How will each of us process and apply God's message now, and throughout life? God has graciously done His part. Ours is to repond. Will we love God back? Obey?

A DISCIPLE'S ASSIGNMENT

Once we have cast our lot with Jesus of Nazareth, we are committed to a life of sharing our Lord with those whose lives we touch. We are urged to be disciples who "teach others who will teach others," so that the torch of faith will not flicker out, but be passed on throughout the generations. Physical generations span many decades, but a spiritual generation does not need to take a lifetime. People can be spiritually born and start moving toward maturity as soon as the Spirit of God is given cooperation in a life. We're urged to play our part in the maternity ward and the pediatric ward of our generation's spiritual experience. To be equipped to be used of the Spirit in such marvelous ways involves knowing and deeply understanding God's word.

As you study "The Messiah Mystery," you have one tool in your hands for becoming familiar with the scriptures, for opening yourself up to depths of meaning, and for gaining new tools you can use to help others be blessed through the written and living Word of God.

MY "LAYERED TEACHING FILE"?

You are encouraged to build your own teaching file gleaned from studying "The Messiah Mystery," using its tools, and being motivated to search the scriptures in your own ways. It is simple to get a loose-leaf notebook (or file folders) in which to keep the various "systems" you study. In them you can store the Circles and Discussion notes and Focus Pages referred to in the KEYS, Part III, plus other handouts and resources you have located or created. Endless resources are available from articles, Bible handbooks, commentaries, audio and videotapes, and in this generation, resources on the web. Visual representations, charts, overviews, and summaries are particularly helpful.

The leader should be careful about attribution. The handouts should always note the author or source, which is only intellectually honest. Copied pages are to be used for educational purposes, never for commercial sale. In days when self-appointed authorities appear on the web without ways to check their credentials, vigilance in evaluating the source and the truth of web material is vitally important.

Over time, you can add your gleanings by general topics, or by periods in biblical history. This is a way to build your own "apologia" with the sources God puts at your disposal. You can help others uncover the marvelous mystery of the Messiah's identity and His meaning, the key to life! Having "done your homework," with John you can confidently proclaim, that "these things are written that you may believe that Jesus is the Christ, the Son of God, and that believing you may have life in his name." May your commitment and your faithfulness result in gems on the altar, to the praise of His glory!

A SAMPLE FROM OUR CREATOR'S "LAYERED TEACHING FILE"

If we need a precedent for helping people learn through layers of meaning, just look at the pattern God gave Moses for the Tabernacle and the Feasts unto the Lord. Talk about a layered treasury! Think about it. His two hallowed PLACES and seven TIMES provided His community with layers of meaning and experience that seem to be inexhaustible and endless.

The experiences around the Tabernacle and Temple, at feast times especially, were intricate and broad, hourly and yearly, sense-based and heart-confronting. Think of the Tabernacle pattern God gave, with all its services and specifications. God directs its geometry – its shape, measurements, weights, and compass points. He layers its beauty – its skins, fabrics, colors, textures, needlework, and inspires its silversmith creations. He brings forth grains and fruits, uses woods and precious metals and gems. He draws in the whole community – animals and men. He employs the elements – earth, water, and fire. He orders the community's space arrangements, time appointments, and Levitical service assignments. Ceremonies, relationships analogies, symbols, meanings, concepts – they all flow out of His amazing "layered teaching file," and they are indelibly memorable and transferable.

God directed the Israelites to create the Tabernacle and Feasts, color them, taste them, smell them, feel them, hear them, value them, watch them, walk them, surround them, carry them, follow them, celebrate them, and remember them – and not just the events, but HIM. Top all that with the mysteries of the Messiah weaving back and forth throughout the whole pattern. Learn some keys to recognizing Yeshua throughout all the scriptures and then stand amazed at our creative God!

ENCOURAGING CREATIVE EXPERIMENTS

Dr. and Mrs. Frances Schaeffer of L'Abri used to insist that God is first of all a Creator, and so it follows that we who are in His image should be creative! God is the Master Teacher. He has poured out His own creativity upon nature and upon man, showering us with myriad forms of communication. They are acts of love.

Our Father has given us all the capacity and gifts to be creative. He has modeled these possibilities throughout the scriptures. He has spelled out His mind and heart in so many ways. Consider His redemptive analogies and their culmination in our Lord's death, resurrection, and ascension. Consider His enjoyment of creation, the rest of the Sabbath, the creation of the Tabernacle, the celebrations of the Hebrew people, the foretaste of the Davidic Kingship, the dramatic acts of the prophets, the Psalms' praises in music and dance, His Son's master story telling, the reasoned arguments of Paul, the living testimonies of the early believers, the marvelous unity of the great pageant of redemptive history, with a Wedding Feast issuing in Eternity!

As grafted-in believers, Gentile Christians can profit by seeing to it that they become familiar with the great storehouse of Hebrew spiritual experience. Broken fellowship over the centuries has cut off Gentiles from the celebrations once experienced in Israel's feasts unto the Lord. God arranged for Jerusalem to be the stage, and Israel to be the players in seven great dramas that would reveal *Adonai's* thoughts and heart to His community. These celebrations in music, dance, color, drama, feasting, and more, would perpetuate their understanding from one generation to another.

We can tap into this pattern through the Bible, and through understanding more about Hebrew culture. We can also create modern-day applications of some of these patterns and principles. In acting out, living out, we learn. We find we can enjoy the process as well, much as children enjoy creative play.

What resources are available along these lines? BOOKS: Alfred Edersheim's Life and Times of Jesus the Messiah is a classic gold mine. Certain publishing companies, such as Kregel, have done a series of Pictorial Guides (to the Bible, to the Tabernacle, and to the Temple). They are handbooks with colored illustrations of biblical times. Martha Zimmerman's Celebrate the Feasts was a catalyst for us. CELEBRATIONS: Martha Zimmerman's book (and many other resources available today) can help Gentiles experiment with the Jewish feasts that God initiated. Of course, even better is to share first hand in those celebrations with Jewish friends. The Jewish community is experienced in expressing joy! FELLOWSHIPS: One example is a season of fellowship between a few individuals from the Jewish and Christian communities in our town, developed by Bonnie Berggren. We learned from each other by celebrating one of the seven "Feasts unto the Lord" at each meeting. The monthly gatherings alternated between various churches and the local synagogue. Our informative studies were based on the biblical feasts and Jewish tradition. Christian interpretations were also shared. TAPES AND VIDEOS: In recent years, Ray Vander Laan has done a series of archeological videotapes on Israel history, adding "faith lessons" in a series called <u>That the World May Know</u>. Many organizations make teaching tapes and videos available for people who want to understand more about the Hebrew roots of Christianity. WEB: Internet resources can add another dimension.

Resources are abundant. However, *simplicity and "hands on" participation* may be more encouraging to creativity than always depending on "spectator" materials. Human beings need both Form and Freedom in their lives. While Form is needed, surely God enjoys our creative experiments, employing Freedom. In our experiments, we've found that doing something, "living it," deepens our capacity to truly believe it. What are some of the "freedoms" with which our particular Messiah Mystery community has experimented? Here are a few:

Turning a mini-life-synopsis of a biblical character into a first-person monologue.
Re-enacting the Egyptian Passover Exodus, at night and outside, families girt to march.
Constructing various models of the Tabernacle.
Attending the Seder with Jewish friends.
Serving Passover Seders at various churches, with a Messianic believer's interpretation.
Doing the Lord's Passover Supper, with our group's men as characters in that drama.
Inviting Jewish-informed teachers to share, or learning from their tapes and videos.
Experimenting as a family with a 24-hour Sabbath in the home.
Writing and performing Messianic-theme plays, such as
    ("Passover + 1 times 7," which dramatizes 7 periods from the Exodus to today.)
    ("A walk-through journey from the Egyptian Passover to the Messiah's Passover.")
    ("Who are we on Good Friday?" – a short play with 10 characters.)
Building outdoor "booths" at the Feast of Tabernacles (especially fun for children).
Doing a Simhat Torah service, casting our stones (sins) into a pond (kids love).
Dedicating an outdoor chapel, dramatized with 12 fathers placing their "Joshua rocks.".
Creating a woodsy amphitheater around a truly rugged cross.
Turning a storm cellar into the empty tomb, visited at dawn on Resurrection morning.
Creating a "Bethlehem Revisited" outdoor pageant at Christmas. (What began as three families' children's original play in a living room eventually grew into a three night outdoor walk-through experience for the town.)

Such "Happenings" take time and effort, but there is something about the creative process and the "hands on" experimentation that encourages the use of our various gifts. It enhances learning, recall, and fellowship. Not expecting such creations to be polished or perfected, we've enjoyed these short "sand paintings," even though they soon fade away on life's shore. They remain in memory! Are we not still informed by God's dramas instituted long ago, still exploring their keys to our Creator's meanings for us today?

Prayer

Now may the God of peace, who brought again from the dead our Lord Jesus, that great shepherd of the sheep, by the blood of the eternal covenant equip you with everything good that you may do his will, working in you that which is pleasing in his sight, through Jesus Christ; to whom be glory for ever and ever. Amen.

Hebrews 13:20, 21

ORDERING INFORMATION

"THE MESSIAH MYSTERY"

and

"KEYS TO THE MESSIAH MYSTERY"

may be requested from local bookstores
or
ordered on line
from
Amazon.com or Barnes & Noble.com